"The Christian counseling world has waited a long time for a book that has substantive help for people weighed down with problems from their past. It's finally here! Steve Viars takes a difficult issue and, aptly and with clarity, applies practical theological answers to it. You cannot read this book without being changed. If you are looking for solid biblical answers about your past, this is the book for you."

—Dr. John D. Street, chair of the Master of Arts in Biblical Counseling program, The Master's College and Seminary

....

"The gospel promises believers the power to change, but those who've experienced deep pain in their past often struggle with living by faith. *Putting Your Past in Its Place* offers practical, compassionate, biblical help for those with painful personal histories, and for their pastors and counselors."

—Dr. Laura Hendrickson, author, biblical counselor, psychiatrist

....

"Steve Viars is a pastoral psychologist of the best sort: realistic, practical, and thoroughly Christian. His book really does put the past in its proper place and does so by comforting, challenging, and encouraging those who need to make peace with their past. Whether you are struggling with the past yourself or someone who counsels the strugglers, you cannot read this book and not be changed."

—Sam R. Williams, PhD, associate professor of counseling, Southeastern Baptist Theological Seminary

....

"Many of us remain paralyzed by our past even though freedom from our past was purchased on the cross. In this much-needed book, Steve Viars shows that the Bible teaches us what we need to know about learning from and disarming our past. So read well, see yourself, see Jesus, and receive His liberating grace."

—Paul Tripp, president, Paul Tripp Ministries and author of *What Did You Expect? Redeeming the Realities of Marriage*

....

"If you long to get free from your past and into the glorious future God has for you, Steve Viars's wonderful new book can show you the way. It is insightful, powerful, and immensely practical. Get one for every member of your family so they can join you in this bright new future free from the pain of your past."

—Dr. James MacDonald, senior pastor of Harvest Bible Chapel

....

"*In Putting Your Past in Its Place*, biblical counselor and Bible scholar Steve Viars seeks to answer the important question, What role does a person's past play in his or her present-day living? Viars bases his answer not on his opinion but on God's authoritative, infallible Word. This interesting and insightful book will be of great benefit to many. Counselors will find it to be very helpful, as will Christians who struggle with discerning a biblical perspective."

—Wayne Mack, professor of biblical counseling, Grace School of Ministry

....

"Steve Viars is thoroughly biblical, pleasantly practical, and sets the record straight about how to handle your past in a God-honoring way. I challenge you to read this book with your past in mind—then put your past in its place so you can help others do the same."

—Garrett Higbee, executive director of Twelve Stones Ministries and team leader of counseling ministry, Harvest Bible Chapel

....

"Steve Viars knows that the answers to our problems are found in the Bible. In *Putting Your Past in its Place,* he takes his wealth of experience in the pulpit and in the counseling room and applies it to the difficulties faced by those who feel shackled to their past. If you want to put your past in its proper place, then this book is for you. It is thoroughly biblical, deeply compassionate, and engagingly hopeful. Buy it!"

—Elyse Fitzpatrick, head of Women Helping Women Ministries and author of *Overcoming Fear, Worry, and Anxiety*

....

"Steve Viars has written this compassionate, biblical, and practical guide to help us avoid the extremes of either dismissing the past or being defined by it. Viars shows us how to face the past with a sympathetic Savior who both suffers with us, offering healing and hope, and also forgives us completely of our sins, offering a clean conscience free from guilt and shame."

—Mike Wilkerson, Biblical Living pastor, Mars Hill Church, and author of the forthcoming book *Redemption*

....

"Steve Viars suggests four ways of considering our past that are fresh, insightful, and hope-giving. The real-life stories clearly model how Christ and His Word are pivotal in understanding our past and our future potential. I was helped by reading this book, and now I have a wonderful new tool to use in helping others!"

—Randy Patten, executive director, National Association of Nouthetic Counselors (NANC)

....

"This book is for anyone whose past impacts their present. Steve Viars demonstrates how the Bible gives us everything we need to not just *understand* our past, but also how to *deal* with it, and more importantly, how to *face the future* with hope. Through Steve's use of clear illustrations, helpful stories, and careful exegesis, readers will be comforted and renewed as they consider their past and make plans for their future."

—Kevin Carson, Biblical counseling department chair,
Baptist Bible Graduate School

....

"Page after page of wisdom, compassion, and understanding await those who use *Putting Your Past in Its Place* to address past hurts."

—Sam Hodges, executive producer, Church Initiative

....

"For a biblical, balanced, discerning, practical, and encouraging discussion of how to deal with one's past, *Putting Your Past in Its Place* is a must-read. Steve Viars draws from counseling cases and personal experience to form biblically reasoned conclusions about how we deal with past sin and suffering in a way that frees us to live in grace rather than being enslaved in self-pity, anger, and bitterness."

—A. Charles Ware, president, Crossroads Bible College

....

"Based on years of pastoral ministry, Steve Viars develops an approach to the past that neither maximizes nor minimizes its importance in the life of the believer. Rather, he sets forth a biblically rich and well-illustrated third way that addresses past suffering and past sin and provides gospel-laden hope for the present and the future."

—Michael R. Emlet, faculty and counselor,
Christian Counseling and Educational Foundation and
author of *CrossTalk: Where Life and Scripture Meet*

....

"Steve Viars offers a biblical, practical, and hope-filled book that is a must-read for all! Whether you are a friend wanting to help a friend, someone looking for victory over serious past issues, or a full-time pastor/counselor in the Master's service, you will find *Putting Your Past in Its Place* an insightful and invaluable resource for real change by God's grace and for His glory."

—Stuart Scott, associate professor of Biblical counseling,
The Southern Baptist Theological Seminary

....

"Steve Viars's biblical input, his sound advice, his illustrations from his own life and others, and his effective pastoral counsel all combine to make this easily the best book on coming to grips with your past. What's better, this book moves you past your past and into your present with a challenge to experience a robust faith in Christ, a sure hope in our heavenly Father, and a fervent love for the Holy Spirit and His truth. Where do you look when your past haunts you? Look no further! Viars's book will be of immense help as you work at *Putting Your Past in Its Place.*"

—Lance Quinn, pastor-teacher,
the Bible Church of Little Rock

....

"We take risks when we share our past with someone. Whether we reveal shameful sins or oppressive suffering, we want to trust the person who hears it. My guess is that you will trust Steve Viars in just the first couple pages. He knows suffering from his own experience and as a veteran pastor who has loved many sufferers. You'll get lots of Scripture. You'll meet people like yourself. And since our pasts can be complicated and muddled, you will quickly appreciate that he is so clear."

—Edward T. Welch, faculty and counselor,
Christian Counseling and Educational Foundation

....

"Theologically sound and pastorally wise, Steve Viars brings the weighty truths and life-changing stories of Scripture to tackle the gnawing problems of both our past sins and our past sufferings. Who would have thought that the Bible could so richly help us reframe our troubled past to bring order to our present and hope for our future?"

—Robert D. Jones, author, assistant professor of Biblical counseling,
Southeastern Baptist Theological Seminary

....

"Many books have been written to help people deal with the hurt and scars of the past, but few have been written from a biblical perspective by an author who has experienced the pain he writes about. As a long-term biblical counselor and pastor, Steve Viars brings a different perspective to this issue, and the metaphors he uses to explain the process of healing may be of great help to you."

—Ed Bulkley, president, International Association of Biblical Counselors

....

Putting Your Past in Its Place

STEPHEN VIARS

Unless otherwise indicated, all Scripture quotations are from the New American Standard Bible®, © 1960, 1962, 1963, 1968, 1971, 1972, 1973, 1975, 1977, 1995 by The Lockman Foundation. Used by permission. (www.Lockman.org)

Verses marked ESV are from The Holy Bible, English Standard Version, copyright © 2001 by Crossway Bibles, a division of Good News Publishers. Used by permission. All rights reserved.

Verses marked KJV are from the King James Version of the Bible.

Cover design by Koechel Peterson & Associates, Inc., Minneapolis, Minnesota

Cover photo © iStockphoto / Thinkstock

Backcover author photo by Personal Touch Portrait Studios

This book contains stories in which the author has changed people's names and some details of their situations in order to protect their privacy.

PUTTING YOUR PAST IN ITS PLACE

Published by Harvest House Publishers
Eugene, Oregon 97402
www.harvesthousepublishers.com

Library of Congress Cataloging-in-Publication Data

Viars, Stephen, 1960-
Putting your past in its place / Stephen Viars.
p. cm.
ISBN 978-0-7369-2739-0 (pbk.)
1. Christian life. 2. Change (Psychology)—Religious aspects—Christianity. I. Title.
BV4509.5.V49 2011
248.8'6—dc22

2010015986

Printed in the United States of America

18 19 20 21 22 / BP-NI / 14 13 12 11 10

To Harry and Carol, who paid for my last seminary class as a congratulatory gift, not realizing Kris and I had no idea how we would pay for it ourselves.

I can still remember Harry's response to our thanks in that trademark East Coast brogue:

"Aw, don't worry about it— just dedicate your first book to me."

Gracious friends who believe in you are a blessing from the Lord.

Contents

Foreword

Pastor Steve Viars has devoted his life and ministry to helping others change—biblically. You hold in your hands the result of his lifelong ministry—Pastor Viars's opus.

It's an opus well worth reading and applying. Whether you're struggling with the process of change related to past suffering or to past sin, *Putting Your Past in Its Place* provides the seasoned, compassionate, pastoral, hope-filled, biblical wisdom you need.

Christians who attempt to address the crucial topic of the past tend toward extremes. Not Steve. He carefully avoids the "past is nothing" and "the past is everything" mind-sets. He scripturally avoids the "truth only" or "love only" approach. Instead, like the apostle Paul, he offers you both the Scriptures and his own soul (1 Thessalonians 2:8).

Steve is a master communicator, having honed the skill of relating God's truth to people's lives through decades as a pastor and biblical counselor. Those skills are on display throughout *Putting Your Past in Its Place.* It provides a comprehensive practical theology of the past that reads like a real-life narrative. Because it is real life—our lives as we deal daily with our past. His creative illustrations, engaging stories, personal examples, weaving in of Jill's story, real-life testimonials, and questions for personal reflection and group discussion all result in the most reader-friendly counseling book you'll ever find.

While I highly recommend *Putting Your Past in Its Place* to the person in the pew, I'm also convinced that it will be a theory-altering, practice-changing book for pastors and biblical counselors. Steve models the sufficiency of Scripture for everyday life like no one I have read. Pastors and counselors can learn from Steve not only how to help their parishioners and counselees to deal with the past, but even more, how to view and use the Scriptures to develop a theology and methodology for dealing with any life issue.

I've known Steve since we were both in elementary school. Given the intensity of his ministry responsibilities, I've wondered how he lives such a joy-filled, hopeful life. I've pondered how he maintains such healthy relationships. Now I know the rest of the story. Steve keeps his accounts current with God. He practices what he teaches. If you want to find God and experience the joy, hope, and love that He offers in Christ, then practice what Steve teaches in this book.

Robert W. Kellemen, PhD,
founder and CEO of RPM Ministries,
professor-at-large for Capital Bible Seminary,
author of *God's Healing for Life's Losses*

Section One

The Power of the Past

Chapter One

Can You Hear the Wheels Spinning?

Have you ever been stuck? One of the jobs I had while going through Bible college and seminary was building in-ground swimming pools. The owner of the business sold the pools and then paid me a set price to perform the installation. I in turn hired the labor, paid for the materials, and collected payments from the customer. Whatever was left after all the bills were paid was my salary.

If everything went well, we could build one pool per week. But one summer we were dramatically behind that pace. It was starting to look as though I might not be able to afford to return to school in the fall.

In early August the owner of the company came to me with one last job on the far north side of Chicago that had the possibility of netting a nice profit for both of us. The challenge was that it was too far away to drive back and forth from home each day. My solution was to borrow my dad's little camper that sat inside a pickup truck. I planned to find some sort of campground near the customer's house and live at the campground for the week.

The first day we arrived on the job, the homeowner offered to let us leave the camper in his backyard, so that is what we did. We took down a few sections of their wood fence and stacked them in the back corner of the yard. Then we pulled the truck all the way in and unloaded the camper next to the pieces of fence.

We dug the hole, which took up a significant percentage of the yard, and began building the pool. About midweek, it started raining and continued for the next seven days. By now I had missed the date I was supposed to return to school, but I had to finish the job.

Finally the weather broke, and we started working. It was a muddy mess, but we slogged through as hard as we could. It was a happy day when we finally completed the pool and started filling it with water. All that was left was to pick up the tools, retrieve the camper, and head for home.

We started to drive the truck around the new pool, but after all the rain, the dirt around the pool was nothing but slippery mud. The tires simply could not get any traction. There we stood, looking over the new pool to the back corner of the yard where my dad's camper sat. When I close my eyes, I can still hear the sound of those wheels hopelessly spinning. There are few things worse than being stuck.

Stuck

You might feel like that. Many men and women have relationships filled with habits they wish would go away. Like the spouse who promised to communicate better but just lashed out with biting sarcasm, again. Or the father who wants to be more positive but just yelled at his child, again. Or the single person who wants to be pure but just fell into immorality, again. Could the past have anything to do with it?

It goes further. There are the private failures. Another night of Internet pornography. Another trip to the liquor store. Another purging session after dinner. Like Jeremiah's leopard that cannot change its spots, such persons are exhausted from promising and failing over and over again. Could the past have anything to do with it?

But the worst is being stuck *in the heart.* Bitterness. Jealousy. Revenge. Rage. Disappointment. Hatred. Lust. Wrath. Discouragement. Fear. Worry. Many persons have thoughts and desires that are both loathsome and familiar. They know they should think differently but such patterns feel like home.

Perhaps you can relate to men and women who hate those words—*stuck...again.* I know I can. The sound of the rotating wheels of an unchanging life can be frustrating, mocking, and hopeless. Could the past have anything to do with it?

Being stuck is a topic for everyone. No one has mastered the process of change. Regrettably some have even stopped trying. They have concluded that substantive change and the hope it brings for the future is beyond their grasp.

But surely the God of heaven disagrees. For men and women struggling with past suffering, God stands ready as "the Father of mercies and God of all comfort, who comforts us in all our affliction" (2 Corinthians 1:3-4). People struggling with sin in the past can take heart that the apostle Paul, after listing a series of behaviors such as greed, sexual unfaithfulness, and drunkenness, says, "But such were some of you" (1 Corinthians 6:11).

My prayer is that this book helps you move from "I am stuck in my pain" to "I have found comfort in God" and from "I did it again" to "such were some of you." I believe handling the past biblically often plays an important role in taking those steps.

What Can You Do?

People like you and me tend to drift between two extremes when considering this subject.

Believing the past is nothing. Just do right. Suck it up. Serve more. The abuses of the past have nothing to do with your choices today. Jump through the right behavioral hoops and you will soon be fine. Your former failures are irrelevant to today's struggles. Don't worry; be happy.

Believing the past is everything. You fail today because you were abused in the past. Your love cup is only half full. Your deep personal needs were not adequately met. Your wounded inner child is creating emotional pain. Your memories need to be healed. Today's choices are not your fault because you are being ruthlessly driven by the past.

Both extremes are problematic for students of Scripture. If *the past is nothing,* then why did God create us with the ability to remember? Why are there so many examples in the Bible of men and women whose past choices dramatically affected their present behavior? Why are we instructed, for example, to not let the sun go down on our wrath (Ephesians 4:26) if today isn't going to affect tomorrow?

Simple religious behaviorism leaves thoughtful people feeling frustrated and unsatisfied, like eating chocolate cake on an empty stomach. Busyness and activity cannot drown out the cries of a hurting heart.

But *the past is everything* view is equally troubling. The Scripture does not encourage us to view ourselves as hopeless victims whose choices today are outside our ability to understand or change. Thinking the problems of life are primarily everyone else's fault may make us feel better in the moment, but is it true?

People who follow such secular concepts often find the relief short-lived and disappointing. To the people of God, ideas from the world are an uncomfortable fit.

A Way Forward

In this book I offer what amounts to a third way. The goal is to craft a biblical theology of the past on a practical, understandable level. I hope to lead us through a study of what God's Word says about how to

- replace guilt and despair with forgiveness and hope
- distinguish aspects of our pasts that are truly different
- unplug the negative effects of a guilty past
- turn failures into stepping-stones for growth
- evaluate the place of the past in current struggles and find hope in the midst of the process
- develop a biblical response to times in the past when we have been hurt, abused, or sinned against
- experience the joy that comes from viewing hard times God's way

- appreciate the sovereignty of God, who can use the past as a marvelous opportunity to teach valuable and life-changing lessons
- be better prepared to help others who are struggling with the past

How Do You Know if This Book Is Right for You?

This topic has universal appeal because every person has a past. We may be different in many ways, but having a past is something we all share in common. It might be one that is primarily positive or primarily negative. It might be one that we remember well or can hardly remember at all. Regardless, we all have one. It would be wise, and perhaps appealing, for each of us to learn how to handle this faculty we all possess. Those who could profit from learning to handle the past well include

- individuals who experience worry, anger, fear, and discouragement in ways and at times that seem to be out of place, senseless, and confusing
- married persons who have habits of relating to their spouses that are destructive, confusing, and long-standing
- persons who are troubled by the abuses of the past. They often relive hurts and mistreatment. They find themselves living with underlying sadness, fear, confusion, rage, emptiness, and pity.
- people who wallow in a guilty past by endlessly reviewing their sins. These people tend to avoid relationships for fear that someone will discover who they are or what they've done.
- individuals who are stuck in a sinful behavior pattern and cannot understand why that style of sinning is so enticing
- parents who want to raise their children well but are modeling and involved in behaviors they swore they would never develop

- single people who fear that their past is preventing them from finding fulfillment in a marriage relationship. Their clock is ticking and there are fewer and fewer prospects.
- counseling practitioners who wish to develop a more comprehensive theology of the past

Opening Salvos

As I have discussed this project with a number of friends and colaborers, they have raised several excellent questions. Some people have even wondered about the foundational presuppositions of this study. Because you may have similar questions, it might be wise to answer a few of these fundamental queries at this point in the discussion.

Aren't Christians supposed to forget "the things which are behind"?

You probably recognize that language from Philippians chapter 3. In this marvelous passage of Scripture, the apostle Paul explains that even though he had many reasons to put confidence in his own righteousness, he knew that his human accomplishments were unable to reconcile him to our Holy God (3:4-7).

Instead, he chose to rest and rejoice in the finished work of Jesus Christ on the cross. His hope was firmly grounded in his resurrected Savior whose righteousness is imputed to the account of every person who repents and believes (3:9).

It was in that context that Paul later said, "Brethren, I do not regard myself as having laid hold of it yet; but one thing I do: forgetting what lies behind and reaching forward to what lies ahead, I press on toward the goal for the prize of the upward call of God in Christ Jesus" (3:13-14).

The phrase "forgetting what lies behind" refers to any of his former righteous deeds that could be used as reasons to believe he should be accepted into God's family on his own merit. After Paul came to understand the doctrine of the holiness of God and the utter sinfulness of man, he then realized that salvation was by grace alone, through faith alone, in Christ alone. He therefore counted his former pedigree as "rubbish" (v. 8).

That is the aspect of his past that he was choosing to forget. Paul is not suggesting that we simply ignore all aspects of our pasts. His point is that we should avoid the tendency to view our own righteousness as a means of sanctifying grace. By taking his focus off himself and his own works, he was able to gaze affectionately at the beauty and sufficiency of his Savior.

Is thinking about the past really biblical?

I commend anyone who has this concern. The Christian life is focused on carefully discerning the truth. Our whole being is involved in this process, as Martyn Lloyd-Jones so helpfully explains,

> Truth comes to the mind and to the understanding enlightened by the Holy Spirit. Then having seen the truth the Christian loves it. It moves his heart. If you see the truth about yourself as a slave of sin you will hate yourself. Then as you see the glorious truth about the love of Christ, you will want it, you will desire it. So the heart is engaged. Truly to see the truth means that you are moved by it and that you love it. You cannot help it. If you see the truth clearly, you must feel it. Then that in turn leads to this, that your greatest desire will be to practice it and to love it.[1]

I would encourage you to ask the Lord to give you a discerning spirit as you read these pages. "Is that really biblical?" is a wise way to interact with any view you encounter.

To answer our question in an introductory way, let's ask Paul, Naomi, Zaccheus, and Onesimus. You probably recognize those names from Scripture. Did the past have anything to do with their stories?

Let's ask Paul

Consider Paul's powerful explanation of what he labeled a "thorn in the flesh" in 2 Corinthians 12. Something had happened repeatedly in Paul's past that had been a source of great pain and suffering for him.

Some Bible teachers have suggested that the thorn was not "in the flesh" but "*for* the flesh."[2] Paul believed that God had allowed some kind of suffering in his past to actually promote his spiritual growth, development, and ministry. Paul also explains that Satan was involved in this process because the thorn was "an instrument of Satan to torment me" (12:7).

This passage is amazing in part because of what is *not* said. Paul never tells his readers the identity of the thorn, an omission that has fueled speculation among Bible students for centuries. Paul also refuses to give Satan center stage in the story. Contrary to those who advocate power encounters as the way to deal with the pain of the past, Satan is given only a passing reference in this text.

Why these omissions? Paul has learned to focus on and rejoice in something (or *Someone*) far more important than the pain of the past. After he repeatedly asked the Lord to remove the thorn, God responded, "My grace is sufficient for you, for power is perfected in weakness" (12:9a).

Even though it was likely this thorn would be an ongoing and perhaps lifelong struggle, Paul drew this incredible conclusion about the pain of the past, "Most gladly, therefore, I will rather boast about my weaknesses, so that the power of Christ may dwell in me. Therefore I am well content with weaknesses, with insults, with distresses, with persecutions, with difficulties, for Christ's sake; for when I am weak, then I am strong" (12:9b-10).

Paul concluded that the suffering in his past had been used of God to make him a stronger and more Christ-centered man.

Let's ask Naomi

Contrast the way Paul related to the difficulties of his past to the tender story of a woman named Naomi. The curtain opens in the Old Testament book of Ruth to the horrifying news that during a time of famine in Israel, Naomi's husband and two married sons die in the country of Moab, where they had gone to live. That part of the story is summarized with these sobering words: "the woman was bereft of her two children and her husband" (1:5).

In the midst of her unspeakable grief, Naomi and her two daughters-in-law, Orpah and Ruth, who were from Moab, set out to return to the land of Judah. At some point along the journey, Naomi encouraged her daughters-in-law to go back to their own people and to their own "gods" (1:15). This statement gives important insight into the way Naomi is processing her grief and despair. For her, Yahweh, the covenant God of Israel, was no better than the gods of the nations.

Even though Ruth had been raised in a different culture and religious system, she respectfully disagreed with her mother-in-law's pluralistic assessment. She said, famously,

> "Do not urge me to leave you or turn back from following you; for where you go, I will go, and where you lodge, I will lodge. Your people shall be my people, and your God, my God. Where you die, I will die, and there I will be buried. Thus may the LORD do to me, and worse, if anything but death parts you and me" (1:16-17).

In the next scene, the two starving widows arrive back in Naomi's homeland, the town of Bethlehem. The imagery is striking in light of the fact that the name *Bethlehem* literally means "house of bread." When the pair enter the city, "all the city was stirred because of them" and the women asked, "Is this Naomi?" (1:19).

Naomi's answer speaks volumes about how she was choosing to respond to the painful suffering of the past:

> "Do not call me Naomi; call me Mara, for the Almighty has dealt very bitterly with me. I went out full, but the LORD has brought me back empty. Why do you call me Naomi, since the LORD has witnessed against me and the Almighty has afflicted me?" (1:20-21).

The Hebrew word *mara* literally means "bitter." In this incredible moment of self-reflection, Naomi summarizes her life by declaring that its defining characteristic was bitterness.

The rest of the book explains that there is a far better way of handling the pain and suffering of the past. Yahweh is truly a superior God who is worthy of one's trust and love even in life's hardest moments. God orchestrates the next events in Ruth's life in a way that is tender and sweet, culminating with a wonderful love story of His faithful provision of a godly husband for her. Ruth was right in choosing the path of steadfast love for the God of Israel. After Ruth and her new husband gave birth to their first child, the women of the city said to Naomi,

> "Blessed is the Lord who has not left you without a redeemer today, and may his name become famous in Israel. May he also be to you a restorer of life and a sustainer of your old age; for your daughter-in-law, who loves you and is better to you than seven sons, has given birth to him" (4:14-15).

As if the story could not get any better, the young baby boy was laid in Naomi's lap, and the tale ends with words that take the breath away from students of God's Word, "The neighbor women gave him a name, saying, 'A son has been born to Naomi!' So they named him Obed. He is the father of Jesse, *the father of David*" (4:17). The great God who provides for His people sovereignly designed these painful events in a way that resulted in this dear family being in the ancestral line of the Great Redeemer, also born in "the house of bread," the Lord Jesus Christ.

Naomi's response to the suffering of her past was far different than the apostle Paul's. That became a significant part of her story. But isn't it wonderful to know that Naomi did not die in bitterness? She eventually saw her past through an entirely different lens and as a result, God's name became famous (4:14).

Let's ask Zaccheus

If you grew up in church, you probably remember the song that immortalizes this story, "Zaccheus was a wee little man..." After Zaccheus believed the message of salvation in Christ, he declared, "Behold, Lord, half of my possessions I will give to the poor, and if I have defrauded anyone of anything, I will give back four times as much" (Luke 19:8).

Zaccheus understood that he had unfinished business from his past. The text is silent on how or why he came up with these formulas, but we can confidently say that Jesus was pleased for He responded, "Today salvation has come to this house, because he, too, is a son of Abraham. For the Son of Man has come to seek and to save that which was lost" (19:9-10).

This does not mean that Zaccheus was saved by making restitution to the people he had robbed because that understanding would contradict so many other places in Scripture that speak of salvation by grace alone through faith (Ephesians 2:8-9). But because Zaccheus had genuinely come to Christ, he realized immediately his past business dealings had to be addressed.

Let's ask Onesimus

Another character in Scripture whose past is a prominent part of the story is Onesimus. An entire book of the Bible, the book of Philemon, is devoted to explaining the process necessary to help this man handle his past.

Onesimus was a runaway slave. He had stolen money from his master, Philemon, and like many runaway slaves sought refuge in the teeming city of Rome. God's sovereignty comes into play once again because Paul knew Philemon and had the privilege of leading him to Christ.

Then God providentially allowed Onesimus to meet Paul, who was imprisoned in Rome. Onesimus became a Christian under Paul's ministry and developed into a very helpful friend (Philemon 10-11).

But Onesimus had unfinished business from the past. Paul, being a man of integrity, understood that those issues had to be addressed if his newfound friend was going to move forward in his walk with Christ. Therefore Paul sent Onesimus back to Philemon with a tender letter urging Philemon to forgive this man who had sinned so grievously, but who was now a brother in Christ. The unaddressed sins of the past had to be and could be dealt with in a way that cleaned the slate between these two men forever.

In considering these four examples, you might respond, "But their stories are far different from one another." Exactly. We will talk about that in more detail in the coming chapters. But if the question is whether it is biblical to speak about the past, the response from Scripture is yes. God's Word does so all the time.

Isn't focusing on the past really just a concept from secular psychology?

That is also a fair question. We live in a day when the people of God often seem enamored with the latest ideas from secular thinkers on how to handle the troubles of life.

I strongly believe in the sufficiency of Scripture. God has given us in His Word all we need to address and solve the nonorganic problems of daily living. (By *nonorganic problems,* I mean problems that are not physical ailments.) "The law of the Lord is perfect, restoring the soul; the testimony of the Lord is sure, making wise the simple" (Psalm 19:7). I agree with Albert Barnes who said about this verse,

> The meaning [of "perfect"] is that [Scripture] lacks nothing [for] its completeness; nothing in order that it might be what it should be. It is complete as a revelation of Divine truth; it is complete as a rule of conduct...It is absolutely true; it is adapted with consummate wisdom to the [needs] of man; it is an unerring guide of conduct. There is nothing there which would lead men into error or sin; there is nothing essential for man to know which may not be found there.[3]

On the other hand, it is undeniable that many secular psychologists have written extensively about the past. Freud based his entire counseling system on this topic. That fact does not automatically disqualify the subject from serious biblical and theological reflection.

Often the writings of secular thinkers can fuel our theology work by driving us back to the Word of God to find answers to the questions people in our culture are posing. Being immersed in a world that often draws unbiblical conclusions should in turn cause us to go back and ask, "What does God's Word say about that?"

How are we defining the word past?

Even in this first chapter, I have used *past* in different ways. That is part of the joy and challenge of communicating in any language.

Ultimately words derive their meaning from their context. I hope the precise way *past* is being used will be apparent in each chapter.

However, as a starting point, the word *past* refers to "the accumulation of events, choices, responses, habits, attitudes, desires, feelings, and beliefs that frame the patterns, interpretations, and routines of our lives today."

Paul was able to come to a new understanding of the grace of God because of the way he responded to the unnamed painful events of his past. Naomi had a heart that was filled with bitterness because of the beliefs she developed about God because of disappointments in the past. Zaccheus understood that his newfound faith in Christ meant that he had unfinished business from the past. And Onesimus learned that hiding out in a busy city would never achieve the freedom from his past that he so desperately needed.

Meet Jill

For over 30 years, our church has had a community-based biblical counseling ministry. Each Monday a group of 25 people, including myself and many members of our pastoral staff, several physicians, educational specialists, and other trained laypersons, step away from our other responsibilities and offer 80 to 100 hours of free biblical counseling to members of our community. We have found this ministry to be a marvelous source of outreach contacts and discipleship opportunities. It also helps our church to position ourselves in our community as people who love men and women who are hurting (Matthew 5:16). We want the people in our town to view our church and its associated ministries as a vital community asset.

It was in that setting that I met Jill. Her name has been changed to protect her identity, but what I share of her story is true. Because Jill has come to believe strongly that God's Word is sufficient in regard to the past, she has been willing to collaborate with me on this portion of the book. Everything that is written about her story has her blessing.

Jill came to our counseling center because of her ongoing battles with depression. She was a young married woman who reported that she had a personal relationship with Jesus Christ and loved her husband and children, but that the depression persisted.

Jill had been to numerous counselors of all stripes over the years from as early as third grade. She had been evaluated by various physicians, and no biological cause of her problems had ever been discovered. She reported that her depression seemed to be more severe during the winter months. She even spoke about times when she struggled with suicidal thoughts. On her intake form she wrote, "I want this to be my last time going to a counselor. After we are through, I want to be able to handle my struggles without falling apart. I want to see them for what they really are and make them go away."

She also wrote, rather cryptically, "I also have acceptance issues." She explained that when she was growing up, she was sent multiple times to group homes, foster homes, and even a psychiatric hospital.

Jill came for counseling in the spring of the year after experiencing an especially difficult winter. Her concern was that if she did not find lasting help, she might not make it through another year.

Could Jill's past have anything to do with her struggles with depression? Was she like Paul or Naomi or Zaccheus or Onesimus? Was her life some sort of combination of all four approaches? Jill and I will try to answer those questions in the coming pages.

Because you should always finish your stories

Meanwhile, back at the pool, my coworkers and I concluded there was no way we were going to get the truck back to the camper. It was way too muddy, and we were sick of listening to those spinning wheels.

They had slung a lot of mud on us as we tried to push the truck, and we were ready to try something new.

That's where Moo-Moo came in. I can't remember exactly how this coworker earned that nickname, but Moo-Moo walked back to the camper and started looking at the wooden fence posts we had removed when we first arrived on the jobsite. Then it all made perfect sense. Ancient Egypt. The pyramids. Wooden fence posts and a marooned camper.

Moo-Moo had us lift up the front of the camper. He then placed two long pieces of wood partially under the camper to form a crude set of railroad tracks. Then he took one of the fence posts and laid it under the camper and across the tracks. Then we repeated the process on the back side of the camper. When we had both ends of the camper sitting on fence posts, it actually rolled. The impact that movement had on us emotionally was amazing. Now we had a plan. Now we had answers. Now we had hope.

We started pushing the camper with all our might, and as it moved forward, we continued to lay down new track and more fence posts. It was an engineering masterpiece as we went from spinning wheels to productive movement. Before long we had the camper out of the mud, loaded on the truck, and on our way home.

There is nothing like the joy of being unstuck.

Maybe It's Your Turn

If you suspect that you may have some unfinished business with your past, there is hope. You are not alone in your struggles. As the apostle Paul explained to the Corinthians, no temptation has overtaken you "except what is common to man" (1 Corinthians 10:13). That means you do not have to remain stuck. Let's roll up our sleeves and see if we can find some fence posts to get you moving again.

Questions for Personal Reflection

1. Do you tend to be a person who believes the past is nothing, or one who believes the past is everything? How does this tendency manifest itself?
2. Can you relate to any of the descriptions under the "How do you know if this book is right for you?" section on pages 17-18? Which one sounded most like you? How and in what ways? For how long?
3. Why did you pick up this book? Is there some part of your story that troubles you? What about your life do you wish never occurred? What about your life today would you like to change?

Questions for Group Discussion

1. Ask a person in the group to share what it feels like to be stuck in an unwanted habit.
2. After reading this chapter, are you more convinced that thinking about the past is a biblical experience?
3. What is your initial impression of Jill? Do you think her past will be an important part of her story?

Chapter Two

Your Past Can Be One of Your Worst Enemies

Most of us have experienced the challenge of moving to a new community and have dealt with the loneliness and fear that attends that experience.

When I was in seventh grade, my parents relocated our family to a town several miles from our previous home. Soon afterward I made a new friend in the neighborhood, and it's fair to say his influence on me was at best a mixed bag. On one hand, he did introduce me to other kids in our subdivision and at my new school. His parents were happy to have me around, and it was a whole lot better than being alone. But he also introduced me to some thoughts and activities that were certainly displeasing to the Lord.

Perhaps you've had someone in your life who was simultaneously your best friend and your worst enemy. Your past can be like that. There is no question that your past can be beneficial to you. We will expand that thought more completely in the next chapter. However, this cluster of experiences, habits, and memories can have a sinister side, especially if you have not handled some aspect of it biblically. It's in that sense that your past can be one of your worst enemies.

What's at Stake?

Some Christians take the position that the past does not matter. They seldom consider how or if prior events might be negatively affecting their current thoughts or behavior. Yet Scripture teaches several ways one's past can have a detrimental impact on the present. Christians who fail to factor such truths into their working theology often run out of behavioral steam because issues of the heart cannot be ignored forever.

Churches can make the problem worse by expecting positive external performance without offering solutions to the pain of disappointment, tragedy, abuse, failure, and suffering. Too often the church suggests and sometimes demands that its people jump through behavioral hoops without providing compassionate and effective care for the inner person. Our message can and must include a robust theology of how the unaddressed issues of the past can possibly have a negative effect today.

Your past can potentially hinder your growth in Christ in at least six different ways. As you read, ask yourself if any of these apply to you.

Unanswered Questions

Think about some of the greatest trials you have faced. You might want to jot them down on a sheet of paper with a list of questions you had as you walked through each experience. What troubled you the most? What was so upsetting? Why do those events still stand out in your memory?

Have you ever asked God?

Have you ever spoken to God about these matters? Really spoken to Him? Have you ever taken time to sit down with a person who is winsome and wise in the things of God to seek answers from Him to the questions that trouble your soul?

Too many people have grown up believing it is wrong to ask God questions. They think such activity is disrespectful, immature, or unfaithful. Of course the ultimate appropriateness of any question involves issues such as content, tone of voice, and heart motivation. But posing questions to God in the right way can actually be an act of reverence and worship because it demonstrates that you want to use the trial of your faith to grow in your understanding of Him.

One man did

Habakkuk was an Old Testament prophet called to minister to the southern kingdom of Judah around 600 BC. This was a significant point in the history of God's people because the northern kingdom of Israel had already fallen to Assyria, but the people of the southern kingdom of Judah had not chosen to repent of their idolatry to avoid the same fate. This lack of godliness on the part of the people of the southern kingdom troubled the prophet deeply.

What Habakkuk chose to do in response is very instructive. The book that bears his name begins,

> How long, O Lord, will I call for help,
> And You will not hear?
> I cry out to You, "Violence!"
> Yet You do not save.
> Why do You make me see iniquity,
> And cause me to look on wickedness?
> Yes, destruction and violence are before me;
> Strife exists and contention arises.
> Therefore the law is ignored
> And justice is never upheld.
> For the wicked surround the righteous;
> Therefore justice comes out perverted.
> (Habakkuk 1:2-4)

Does it surprise you that words like that are in the Bible? Can you picture this conversation taking place? A person looks to heaven and asks why Almighty God has not yet answered him, and why God has allowed His people to continue in their sin without consequences. Habakkuk is sickened by the violence and disobedience around him. Why has God allowed all of this to continue? Commentating on Habakkuk's queries, one writer said,

> God is the friend of the honest doubter who dares to talk to God rather than about him. Prayer that includes an element of questioning God may be a means of increasing one's faith. Expressing doubts and crying out about unfair situations in the universe show one's trust in God and one's confidence that God should and does have an answer to humanity's insoluble problems.[1]

Fortunately, Habakkuk had the courage and wisdom to bring his questions directly to the throne of God. The rest of the book indicates the Lord was honored that His servant was willing to cultivate a relationship with Him that was honest and authentic.

How does God answer?

This is not to suggest that God will somehow audibly answer our questions. In our day and time, God has "granted to us everything pertaining to life and godliness" (2 Peter 1:3) in His sufficient Word (2 Timothy 3:16-17). As we walk in the Spirit, we have every reason to believe that He will give us the wisdom, direction, and answers we need (1 John 2:20-21,27).

The courage to pose such questions to our heavenly Father is what motivates us to go to His Word for answers and guidance. Some of God's people have not taken that step regarding key questions from the past. Presently, for reasons they may not even understand, they grieve the lack of vibrancy in their relationship with Christ.

Could that be you? Is it possible that at a pivotal time in your life you stuffed your questions in the recesses of your heart instead of believing that God would care enough to listen? If so, your past has become your enemy.

Unaddressed Hurts

Life this side of heaven can be incredibly painful. If I have learned anything as a pastor, it is that many men and women bear the scars of being sinned against in terrible ways. Spouses abandon their mates. Parents neglect and sometimes abuse their children. Employers misuse their workers. Religious leaders fail their congregations. The list of possible hurts is practically endless.

Is it wrong to acknowledge pain?

But some people have grown up believing that it is somehow wrong to feel hurt. *Big boys don't cry. Christians are supposed to be happy all the time. Just rub some dirt on it.*

Is that the best the church has to offer? Is such an approach even remotely consistent with God's Word?

Of course not. A good starting point for answering that is the startling revelation that God Himself is capable of a significant range of emotions. His precious Son wept at the tomb of Lazarus (John 11:35) as He considered the effects of sin on the human condition. The Old Testament had promised that the Messiah would be "a man of sorrows and acquainted with grief" (Isaiah 53:3). The people of Israel could take heart because

> In all their affliction He was afflicted,
> And the angel of His presence saved them;
> In His love and in His mercy He redeemed them,
> And He lifted them and carried them all the days
> of old.
>
> (Isaiah 63:9)

Some of God's most devoted followers were man enough to cry. For example, Job openly stated in front of his three supposed counselors, "My face is flushed from weeping, and deep darkness is on my eyelids" (Job 16:16). Regrettably those who came to comfort him made matters worse as they relentlessly suggested that the loss of his children and material possessions was due to his own sin. This led Job to say that "my friends are my scoffers; my eye weeps to God" (16:20).

Developing spiritual candor

In his book *Soul Physicians,* biblical counselor Robert Kellemen writes about the importance of developing spiritual candor, which he defines as courageously telling oneself the truth about life, "in which I come face-to-face with the reality of external and internal suffering." He goes on to say, "In candor, I admit what is happening to me and I feel what is going on inside me."[2] He then reminds the readers of King David's words in Psalm 42:3-5:

> My tears have been my food day and night,
> While they say to me all day long, "Where is
> your God?"
> These things I remember and I pour out my
> soul within me.
> For I used to go along with the throng and
> lead them in procession to the house of God,
> With the voice of joy and thanksgiving,
> a multitude keeping festival.
> Why are you in despair, O my soul?
> And why have you become disturbed
> within me?
> Hope in God, for I shall again praise Him
> For the help of His presence.

Kellemen is right to emphasize the importance of being honest about our hurts. This is an essential part of what it means to be made in the image of God.

Yet how many of God's people have bought the lie that emotions are for sissies or that real Christians never cry? What happens when hurts are never faced? Is it true that time heals all wounds? Author and biblical counselor Wayne Mack wrote,

> "Time heals all wounds" is one of the most inane statements ever made. Spiritual wounds may harden into scabs and scars over time, but their harmful consequences inevitably

> continue unless true healing occurs. Time by itself can never truly heal any wound of a spiritual nature.[3]

Unaddressed hurts can become a powerfully negative part of a person's past. That is why Scripture spends so much time teaching how such hurts can be handled in a way that is thorough and powerful. We will study this subject in much greater detail in later chapters.

Unsolved Problems

Problems that go unresolved often have lingering effects. That is why the Bible instructs us to use the energy created by anger to solve problems with other people before the sun goes down (Ephesians 4:26). We are even warned that failing to do so gives "the devil an opportunity" (4:27).

Are you living in an unreconciled state with someone in your life? Have you concluded that you can live with this condition from your past without being negatively affected today?

Beware of what might spring up

Unsolved problems may be one of the most common ways a person's past has become his enemy. One of the many possible results is bitterness. The writer of Hebrews warns us to "pursue peace with all men, and the sanctification without which no one will see the Lord. See to it that no one comes short of the grace of God; that no root of bitterness springing up causes trouble, and by it many be defiled" (Hebrews 12:14-15).

Note carefully that bitterness is likened to a plant, which begins under the surface of the soil and grows up over time. Even an unkind word or a thoughtless deed can begin this process. Some Christians feel uncomfortable or disconnected from certain people in their life, and they have never taken the time to consider why that is the case.

For others it was something far more significant. The abuse was real or the disappointment was significant. But the issue has never been discussed. The abuser has never been approached even if this step has been wisely counseled by others. The resultant bitterness is as thick and black as old motor oil in a worn-out engine.

Notice also that Hebrews 12:15 says many other people can be "defiled" by bitterness. Entire families have been ruined by an unresolved problem. Churches often split because men and women do not address problems in a biblical and timely fashion. Friend, is it possible that an unsolved problem with another person in your life has made the past your enemy?

Unwise Choices

The past includes both suffering and sinning. Unaddressed events from either category can have a detrimental effect. This includes making unwise choices.

Scripture teaches the cumulative nature of life. The choices you make today become part of who you are, your spiritual DNA. One direct example is Paul's warning to the Corinthians about the residual effects of sexual sin:

> Do you not know that your bodies are members of Christ? Shall I then take away the members of Christ and make them members of a prostitute? May it never be! Or do you not know that the one who joins himself to a prostitute is one body with her? For He says, "The two shall become one flesh." But the one who joins himself to the Lord is one spirit with Him (1 Corinthians 6:15-17).

Paul's point is that exposing your life to certain behaviors begins a cycle of habituation that is often very difficult to break. The upshot is clear. Don't even start. If you've never looked at pornography, don't start. If you've never taken drugs, don't start. If you've never gotten drunk, don't start. If you've never used profanity, don't start.

Paul taught a similar principle to the Galatians when he said, "Do not be deceived, God is not mocked; for whatever a man sows, this he will also reap" (Galatians 6:7). The lesson is, if you don't want to reap it, don't sow it. Of course the lie of the devil is, "You can make certain choices today, and as time rolls on, it won't hurt you." Some of us who are older know how untrue that is.

I realize that some, if not many, readers will say, "But I already started." I'm not suggesting that you can't change as long as you're willing to be honest about the existence of the problem. But if you have operated on the premise that "the past is nothing," you are more likely to make choices today that you'll regret tomorrow.

Unconfessed Sin

Some men and women do not want to think about the past because they do not want to be reminded of their failures. We can be incredibly creative when it comes to devising strategies that help us avoid admitting to God and others, "I sinned; please forgive me."

Adam's approach

Solomon was right when he said there was nothing new under the sun. This refusal to face our sin with grief, brokenness, and repentance is as old as the Garden of Eden. When God confronted Adam about his sin in Genesis 3:9-11, he could have simply said, "I rebelled against Your command and, in so doing, sinned against You. Would You please forgive me?" Adam would have cleared his conscience and put his past behind him.

Instead, Adam said, "The woman whom you gave to be with me, she gave me from the tree, and I ate" (Genesis 3:12). Have you ever considered how outrageous a statement that was? As if Eve held him down and crammed the fruit into his mouth before he could stop her? Think of the irony: Adam was standing in God's beautiful creation and using his God-given creativity to find a way to avoid dealing with his sin.

Eve's approach

Eve was no better: "The serpent deceived me, and I ate" (Genesis 3:13). This aspect of the story might actually be humorous were it not for the stark reminder of how we often deny or shift blame for our failures. The challenge is that those events become part of our past and can continue to hurt us while they remain unresolved. That's why Solomon warned his son, "He who conceals his transgressions will not prosper, but he who confesses and forsakes them will find compassion" (Proverbs 28:13).

Unlearned Lessons

A sixth way the past can be your enemy is when you do not learn the lessons God wants you to learn. You repeat the same mistakes over and over.

In one of the more graphic word pictures in the book of Proverbs, we read, "Like a dog that returns to its vomit is a fool who repeats his folly" (Proverbs 26:11). The principle is this: Bad choices that are not recognized and corrected become part of who we are. Note the key word *repeats.* Each time we sin in our thoughts, words, desires, or behavior makes it easier and more likely that the same wrong choice will be repeated. When we fail to learn lessons, dangerous ruts are created in the road of our hearts.

These habits of the past can become incredibly powerful. Perhaps this is what Jeremiah had in mind when he asked, "Can the Ethiopian change his skin or the leopard his spots?" (Jeremiah 13:23). St. Augustine said,

> Bound as I was, not with another man's irons, but by my own iron will. My will the enemy held, and thence a chain for me, and bound me. For of a forward will, was lust made; and a lust served, became custom; and custom not registered became necessity. By which links, as it were, joined together (whence I called it a chain) a hard bondage held me enthralled.[4]

This is one of the reasons our society uses addiction terminology to describe various behaviors. The choices involved in abusing alcohol, for example, become so well engrained that the person feels unable to control or change the process. The road to the liquor store on payday becomes so well traveled that the addict feels as if the car is driving there of its own initiative. Addicts make statements like, "I felt like I was in a trance as those choices were unfolding," or "I did not want to do it again, but I knew I could not stop." Biblical counselor Ed Welch explains,

> Addicts feel as if they are trapped and out of control. They feel like abject worshippers, devoted to something that can be very dangerous. They feel desperate hunger and thirst for something. They feel like they can't let go, clinging even when the addictive behavior yields very few pleasures and a great deal of pain. They feel like they are in bondage. Addicts feel out of control, enslaved, stuck, and without hope for freedom or escape. Something or someone other than the Living God controls them, and the controlling object tells them how to live, think, and feel.[5]

Where Does This Leave Us?

At this point of our discussion, we are in a similar position to Ebenezer Scrooge after being visited by the three spirits on Christmas Eve. His question was, "Have I seen the shadows of things that *will be,* or are they shadows of things that *may be*?" In one of the more haunting scenes in Dickens's *A Christmas Carol,* the shrouded ghost refuses to answer.

As a Christian, if you find yourself with examples from your past that fit one or more of the categories we have described, take heart. Our God is no faceless apparition with a dark hood and a pointed finger. He is the light of the world, and He stands ready to help us overcome any aspect of our past that is hindering us from moving forward in our relationship with Him.

For Jill

At first Jill was reluctant to talk about her past. It was like a room she preferred not to enter. But gathering data is a key component of biblical ministry. Solomon was right when he said that "he who gives an answer before he hears, it is folly and shame to him" (Proverbs 18:13). The phrase "before he hears" refers to the failure to listen carefully and compassionately to what has already occurred in a person's life. Giving answers about what should occur today without developing an understanding of what transpired yesterday is a sure recipe for counsel that in God's eyes is both foolish and shameful.

The centrality of the heart

Biblical progressive sanctification, the process of changing and growing to become more like Christ, does not singularly focus on practicing right behaviors in the present. Such an approach ignores Scripture's robust explanation of the inner man, often described in God's Word with the summary term *heart.* This word, used over 700 times in the Bible, refers to much more than the seat of the emotions. It includes our thoughts, desires, choices, beliefs, plans, and feelings. Those aspects of our inner man do not appear out of thin air. They have a history and are formulated over time as we process the events of daily living.

The biblical term *heart* is meaningless without making a logical connection to a person's past. "Watch over your heart with all diligence, for from it flow the springs of life" (Proverbs 4:23). Each of us has developed patterns of feeling, desiring, thinking, and choosing in our hearts. Over time that becomes our "manner of life" (Ephesians 4:22) that must be faced and analyzed in light of God's Word. That is part of what Solomon meant when he commanded his sons to "watch over" their hearts "with all diligence."

As Jill became more comfortable with me and the two trainees who were serving as part of our counseling team (I never counsel women alone), she began to tell her story with the level of detail necessary to help all of us gain a better understanding of her depression.

Significant suffering

Jill was not there to gossip about her parents or other people in her life. But she had experienced incredibly painful losses. Her biological parents were divorced when Jill was seven months old. Her biological father married another woman, but Jill seldom saw them.

Jill's biological mother married a man who eventually sexually abused Jill. The abuse began at age 10 and continued throughout her teenage years. When Jill tried to speak to her mother about this, both she and her stepfather claimed she was dreaming.

When Jill was 15 years of age, her mother signed over her parental rights to the state, claiming that Jill was incorrigible. Jill was placed in a state-run detention facility; but on home visits, Jill's stepfather continued to sexually abuse her.

Jill was eventually placed in a foster home, and after a period of time, she confided in her foster-father about the abuse that had occurred. Charges were filed, and eventually Jill's stepfather was arrested and jailed. Within 30 days, Jill's biological mother posted bail for her husband. By then Jill was so depressed that she attempted suicide.

She was placed in a psychiatric hospital and eventually allowed to make a telephone call home. She learned that her mother was planning to take a vacation to Florida with her husband. Jill was outraged at that notion and said, "But you're taking the problem with you." Her mother's response was, "No, you are the problem. You are the one who laid there."

Can you imagine the agony of hearing those words? In a homework assignment I later gave Jill to help me understand that event, she wrote, "I flipped out and had to visit the 'pink room' [the padded room in the hospital for people with suicidal tendencies]. I spent my 17th birthday in the hospital without a card, call, or visit from my parents. I'll never forget it."

I believe it would have been impossible for Jill to progress out of her depression without a careful understanding and biblical interpretation of her past. Listening to her story, both the actual events and her subsequent interpretations and reactions became a crucial part of the process. This has nothing to do with being Freudian. We are talking about gaining enough information to begin to explain what led to Jill's depression. It also gave me an opportunity as Jill's counselor to attempt to represent the Lord Jesus, who stands ready to "sympathize" with us and invite us to His "throne of grace" (Hebrews 4:15-16).

Was the Lord part of her story?

Another important piece of information was that Jill reported that as a child she had been taken to church and had accepted the gospel of Jesus Christ. She subsequently attended church from time to time and considered herself to be a Christian.

What was curious was that she never mentioned God in telling her story. When I asked her to summarize her life as a married mother with two children, the words she used were "depressed" and "abused." Those were the primary lenses she had developed to view and explain her existence.

During that particular counseling session, there was a fair amount of grieving. If there was ever a time for brothers and sisters in Christ to "weep with those who weep" (Romans 12:15), that was it. We wanted Jill to have the freedom to speak openly, without fear of judgment, pat answers, or more rejection, about what it was like to experience such treatment. She seemed to genuinely appreciate having a setting where she could be honest and open about what occurred.

We also began to talk about the heinous nature of sin and its effects on the world. Theologian Cornelius Plantinga was right when he declared in his famously titled book that sin is "not the way it's supposed to be."[6] Jill had suffered deeply at the hands of sinful people and there was no reason to sugarcoat, ignore, or minimize what had transpired.

While this was not the time for lectures or long speeches, we also broached the subject of what God thought about such treatment. He is angry over injustice (Psalm 7:11) and grieves over the sinful nature of His creation (Genesis 6:5-6).

Most importantly, God sent His precious Son to die for sin and reconcile sinners to Himself (Romans 5:8). Although Jill reported that she knew Christ as Savior and Lord, there was little evidence that her relationship with Him affected her past in any practical or meaningful way. She was somewhat like the man of Psalm 10:4, who has concluded "there is no God." Of course she never would have said those words, but her working theology of the past was something close to that.

This was not the time to raise such issues, but we noted Jill's tendency for future conversations. And even beginning to gently mention God's response to the abuse of her past seemed helpful to Jill. Perhaps there was more to her past than "depressed" and "abused."

Charles H. Spurgeon sometimes struggled with bouts of depression. He learned, as the quote below illustrates, that thinking about the way God has demonstrated His character in the past is an important and valuable discipline.

> Oh, there is, in contemplating Christ, a balm for every wound; in musing on the Father, there is a quietus for every grief; and in the influence of the Holy Ghost, there is a balsam for every sore. Would you lose your sorrow? Would you drown your cares? Then go, plunge yourself in the Godhead's deepest sea; be lost in his immensity; and you shall come forth as from a couch of rest, refreshed and invigorated. I know nothing which can so comfort the soul; so calm the swelling billows of sorrow and grief; so speak peace to the winds of trial, as a devout musing upon the subject of the Godhead.[7]

Our time with Jill consisted of far more listening than talking. But even beginning to gently shift Jill's focus from her abuse and depression to a God who deeply cared for her was a step in the right direction. Her past did not have to remain an enemy forever. We had a long way to go, but Spurgeon was right: there is nothing quite like a devout musing on the Godhead.

Questions for Personal Reflection

1. List the five to ten most hurtful events in your past. Have you spoken to God about these and posed the legitimate questions of your heart? Have you studied His Word to find

answers and sought wise counsel? If not, how might these events from your past be negatively affecting you today?

2. Do you have unsolved problems with people in your life? Take a few moments and jot down their names and a description of the event(s) that caused the breach in your relationship. How frequently do you think about these situations? Do they ever affect the way you relate to other people today? Do you have bitterness in your heart toward any of these people?

3. Are there lessons you should have learned in the past but haven't? Has that resulted in habits that plague you even today? Are there any ways in which you, like the person described in Proverbs 26:11, "return to your folly"? What consequences have you faced as a result of allowing certain aspects of your past to remain an enemy? List some of those lessons that should have been learned long ago.

Questions for Group Discussion

1. Why do some people believe it is wrong to pose hard questions to God? Come up with the names of people in the Bible who were willing to openly relate to the Lord even when their hearts were breaking.

2. Does the average church foster an environment in which men and women can be honest about their hurts from the past? Should emotional authenticity or transparency be a goal for a body of believers? Describe what this would look like in your church fellowship.

3. Why is it so hard for us to be honest about our sins? What are some of the games we play to avoid taking responsibility for our actions? How does unconfessed sin in the past negatively impact life in the present?

Chapter Three

Your Past Can Be One of Your Best Friends

I WAS LIKE MOST TWO-YEAR-OLD BOYS: long on wonder for the world and short on caution and balance. By my mom's telling, I was tearing through the house to get from point A to point B. My parents had thoughtlessly purchased end tables and even had the audacity to place them in my racetrack. They called the space something else—"living room" I think. At an inopportune moment, my feet got tangled up and down I went, catching the corner of one table right between my eyes.

It was one of those "by the grace of God" moments because the injury could have been far worse. The wound bled, my mom cried, and I waited impatiently while she wiped me off before I could resume my adventures. As the wound healed, a scar began to form that is still with me today.

Is that not strange? A brief encounter over 40 years ago can have lasting impact as plain as the nose on my face. You too probably have distinguishing features—surgical scars, birthmarks, whatever they might be. They are just part of who you are.

Your past is like that. It has marked you, and in some cases, marked you deeply. If you are like most people, you probably don't think about it very much. But just like the ever-present notch between my eyes, your past is a silent companion that accompanies you wherever you go.

What was God thinking? He could have made us without the capacity to remember. Every day would literally be a new day with no memories, no past, and no baggage.

Would that make life better? If you could walk through a device similar to a metal detector at an airport but one that would erase your past and its effects on you today, would you do it? And would you be better off?

Some people seem to think so. They describe the past with phrases such as "toxic past," "wounded inner child," or "damaged emotions." In many cases they do so with good reason. As a counselor who spends hours each week listening to the experiences of hurting men and women, my heart often breaks over the abusive and painful experiences of others.

But does that mean that the past, in its entirety, is a bad thing? Would we all be better off if we could completely erase our memories and the impact our past has on our lives today?

Not if we allow God's Word to guide us.

The Bible gives us several ways our pasts can be among our best friends. Of course your past is not an "it." It is not a separate entity. But it is a record, in part, of the way God has related to you and worked in your life. The goal is not to focus on "it" but on who God is and what He has done.

As you read the following examples of how the past can be your friend, ask yourself if you are allowing this silent companion to serve you the way God designed. Perhaps there are elements of your past that are like a good friendship waiting to be cultivated and explored.

When You Need Strength and Confidence

Facing a difficult dilemma

Most likely you are familiar with the Bible's account of the encounter between David and Goliath. The armies of Israel were faced off against their archenemy, the Philistines. Each morning and evening a giant warrior named Goliath came out to taunt the Israelites by offering to fight any man they would send. The deal was that if Goliath lost, the Philistines would become Israel's servants. But if Goliath won, Israel would be enslaved to them. First Samuel 17:11 records this somber report: "When Saul and all Israel heard these words, they were dismayed and greatly afraid."

Have you ever faced a challenge that seemed overwhelming? A habit that seemed impossible to break? A person who ridiculed your belief? A threat or insult that threw you off balance? We all have. Most of us know too well what it means to be "dismayed and greatly afraid" because of a seemingly Goliath-sized challenge.

But then the scene changes. Young David is sent by his father to check on his older brothers, who were supposedly "fighting with the Philistines" on the front lines (1 Samuel 17:19). In the providence of God, David arrived just as Goliath came out to offer his morning dose of insults. David heard Goliath's words and was stunned to see that the men of his country "were greatly afraid" (v. 24). He asked, "Who is this uncircumcised Philistine, that he should taunt the armies of the living God?" (v. 26).

David's oldest brother, Eliab, undoubtedly embarrassed by his own fear and inaction, attempted to soothe his guilt by silencing his kid brother. "Why have you come down? And with whom have you left those few sheep in the wilderness? I know your insolence and the wickedness of your heart" (v. 28).

King Saul's condescending response to David's offer to fight Goliath was equally insulting. "You are not able to go against this Philistine to fight with him; for you are but a youth" (v. 33). Imagine the impact these negative words from Goliath, Eliab, and Saul could have had on this young shepherd boy.

Drawing strength from the past

But now it was time for David to introduce his king, his brother, and people like you and me to a quiet but powerful companion: his past. David's words are forever immortalized in Scripture:

> But David said to Saul, "Your servant was tending his father's sheep. When a lion or a bear came and took a lamb from the flock, I went out after him and attacked him, and rescued it from his mouth; and when he rose up against me, I seized him by his beard and struck him and killed him. Your servant has killed both the lion and the bear; and this uncircumcised Philistine will be like one of them, since he has taunted the armies of the living God." And David said, "The Lord who delivered me from the paw of the lion and from the paw of the bear, He will deliver me from the hand of this Philistine" (vv. 34-37).

David purposely and consciously recalled God's blessing in the past. He drew strength and courage from memories of former victories from his God. David had learned to cultivate a right relationship with his past.

Do you ever do that? Have you amassed a mental list of times God strengthened and helped you in days gone by? Can you talk about your bears and lions so you are prepared when a giant comes along?

You might wonder how David developed this skill. Perhaps a hint comes from reading the Psalms David wrote. It is not hard to imagine many of these worship songs being written and sung by a young shepherd on a lonely hillside. Notice how often he recounts God's blessings in the past—especially in situations that we might have labeled "negative," "traumatic," or "harmful." Marvel at his descriptions of God's character and his rejoicing in God's works. To David, the past was his friend.

When You Need Encouragement and Balance

Another hero of the faith who benefitted from his past was Job. The book that bears his name begins by telling us that Job was blameless and upright. He feared God and turned away from evil. He and his wife had been marvelously blessed with seven sons, three daughters, and an incredible amount of wealth.

An onslaught of devastation

The scene turns sinister as Satan comes to God and charges that Job loves God only because of God's blessings. The relationship, according to the adversary, is nothing more than quid pro quo. Then Satan says, "Put forth Your hand now and touch all that he has; he will surely curse You to Your face" (Job 1:11).

It is critical to understand that this was not simply a test of Job. Fundamentally it was a test of God and whether the righteousness and goodness He develops in the heart of His children is self-centered, shallow, and based merely on temporal circumstances.

The stage is set in verse 12 when we read, "Then the LORD said to Satan, 'Behold, all that he has is in your power, only do not put forth your hand on him.' So Satan departed from the presence of the LORD."

From there the story develops in rapid-fire succession. Some of Job's animals are stolen by a band of marauders while others are killed by fire. Then his children, who are feasting together, are killed when a wind comes and destroys the house they are in. In a matter of moments, Job loses much of his wealth and all of his children.

The camera pans back to Job to see if Satan's prediction will come true. But the faith God built in Job stood firm:

> Then Job arose and tore his robe and shaved his head,
> and he fell to the ground and worshiped. He said,
>   "Naked I came from my mother's womb,
>   And naked I shall return there.
>   The LORD gave and the LORD has taken away.
>   Blessed be the name of the LORD."
> Through all this Job did not sin nor did he blame God.
> (Job 1:21-22)

Now all Job has left is his wife and his health, until chapter 2 reports that Satan "went out from the presence of the LORD and smote Job with sore boils from the sole of his foot to the crown of his head" (v. 7). The climax comes when Job's wife says, "Do you still hold fast to your integrity? Curse God and die!" (v. 9).

A reservoir of hope

At that very point Job, like young David, turns to a familiar friend—his past. He says to his wife, "Shall we accept good from God and not accept adversity?" (v. 10).

Job had a ready list of all the ways God had blessed him and his family in days gone by. They had enjoyed tremendous wealth. They had shared many marvelous times together. God's goodness was rich and abundant.

Did that erase the current trials? Of course not. Does it suggest that spiritual people do not grieve honestly and deeply? No, because Job vividly models the skill of practicing spiritual candor.

I am also not suggesting that Job perfectly followed this principle throughout the rest of the story. Who would have? But this is the critical point: At that moment, rehearsing the past helped him face the present with balance and encouragement. Doing so allowed him to greatly honor his God and to minister to his wife at a time when she desperately needed his spiritual leadership, strength, and love.

We would do well to think about David and Job. Is it not amazing that at critical stages in their spiritual journey they both chose to benefit from their pasts? They had cultivated a purposeful connection to their pasts that was so habitual that they almost automatically factored it into whatever they were facing at the time. Like any good friend, their pasts served them well.

Careful readers will recognize that what we are really talking about here is thanksgiving. Both Job and David developed the discipline of acknowledging God's blessing and continually building a reservoir of memories and lessons from which to draw.

However, God's blessings and goodness in the past are relevant only if we allow them to be. Think about the last trial you faced. Was your response to the trial truly balanced? I am not suggesting that you minimize the loss or paste a plastic smile on a broken heart, but would it have been appropriate to follow in the footsteps of Job (2:10) and temper the pain of the present trial by recounting God's goodness in the past?

Perhaps this is what the apostle Paul meant when he made the outlandish suggestion, from prison no less, that we should be people who "rejoice in the Lord always" (Philippians 4:4). He went on to teach that we should "be anxious for nothing" (v. 6). Then he explained that we can live this way if we learn to pray with thanksgiving (v. 6b). Thanksgiving for what? For God's goodness and blessing in the past.

Cultivating this kind of heart and lifestyle is challenging, to say the least. But consider the end result. "And the peace of God, which surpasses all comprehension, will guard your hearts and your minds in Christ Jesus" (v. 7).

When You Need the Ability to Forgive

The examples we have considered thus far suggest that crucial qualities such as strength, confidence, encouragement, and balance are dependent in part on learning to benefit from our pasts the way God designed. But that is not the end of the story. The way you relate to your past will even affect how well you practice the all-important skill of forgiveness.

In Matthew 18, Jesus taught His disciples how to respond if a fellow believer sins. The process, commonly referred to as church discipline, is a beautiful expression of the character of God. This is especially true because the goal for everyone involved is restoration and forgiveness.

At a crucial point in the discussion, Peter asked how many times he should be willing to forgive a person who had sinned against him. Not wanting to appear too unspiritual, he even upped the rabbinic teaching that you had to forgive up to three times when he asked, "Up to seven times?" (Matthew 18:21). Imagine Peter's shock when Jesus said, "Up to seventy times seven."

But then Jesus told a parable intended to help Peter and the rest of us learn how to forgive others as often as they ask. The Lord spoke of a king who decided to settle his accounts with his slaves. A man who owed the king 10,000 talents was brought before the king. That enormous amount of money was much more than he could ever hope to repay. The king commanded that the slave be sold along with his family and earthly belongings.

The slave fell on his knees and begged the king to be patient with him and promised to repay all the debt. Of course that was impossible, but the king "felt compassion and released him and forgave him the debt" (Matthew 18:27).

But that's not the end of the story. Jesus explained that the forgiven slave found a fellow slave who owed him 100 denarii, or about a third of a year's salary for a typical laborer. Though a sizeable amount of money, it was small in comparison to the vast sum the first slave had already been forgiven. But amazingly, he seized his fellow slave, choked him, and demanded immediate payment. The second servant then made the identical request: "Have patience with me and I will repay you" (v. 29). But the first man refused and had his fellow slave thrown in prison.

The other slaves in the parable recognized this man's ingratitude and reported his harsh actions to the king, who said, "You wicked slave, I forgave you all that debt because you pleaded with me. Should you not also have had mercy on your fellow slave, in the same way that I had mercy on you?" (v. 33).

There was little question about Jesus' point to Peter or to us. Your willingness to forgive is directly related to your remembering how much God has forgiven you. Perhaps that's one of the reasons Jesus instructed His followers to celebrate regularly the Lord's Table. When Christians gather together around the bread and wine, we are reminded, among other things, of the tremendous price Jesus paid to secure our redemption and the tremendous forgiveness extended to us. That leads to an appropriate and joyful celebration of the resurrection and the new life we enjoy in Christ. The beauty and significance of this practice is diminished if we forget why the body and blood were necessary.

If you are having trouble forgiving someone who hurt you, it may be time to sit down and revisit the ways God has forgiven you. In so doing, your past will become a more helpful friend.

When You Are Struggling with Pride

Many of us wrestle with the sin of pride. We tend to place a fairly high value on our opinions, positions, and performance. It was with good reason that Paul instructed the Romans to "be of the same mind toward one another; do not be haughty in mind, but associate with the lowly. Do not be wise in your own estimation" (Romans 12:16).

One way we can avoid this sin is to properly benefit from recalling our sins from the past. This does not mean we should wallow around in them (we will deal with that tendency later in this book). But if the Word of God is going to be our guide, there are clearly times when it is proper for us to remember the ways we have failed.

Consider this example: Just prior to entering the promised land, Moses told the children of Israel, "Remember, do not forget how you provoked the Lord your God to wrath in the wilderness; from the day that you left the land of Egypt until you arrived at this place, you have been rebellious against the Lord" (Deuteronomy 9:7).

Most of us are much better at remembering the failures of others than we are at remembering our own failures. If you are a parent, you probably deal regularly with the ways your child needs to change. Some parents lecture or discipline their children in a manner that is proud and condescending. But parents who are properly connected to the past respond to their children through the lens of "you sinned, but I have sinned too." This approach produces grace and a mutual walk to the cross. Pride can be very destructive in parenting. Mothers and fathers who let their struggles from the past develop patient humility with their children are more likely to enjoy relationships that are authentic and helpful.

Developing this skill can also help you reach out to people in your church and community who have made messes of their lives. Some congregations adopt the attitude, "We don't want that kind of person around here." They become houses of rejection instead of havens of grace. The members of such churches have forgotten all the ways they failed. That makes them poor stewards of their pasts.

When It Is Time to Repent

Many Christians could not tell you the last time they asked another person's forgiveness. We are often incredibly unskilled in the matter of repentance. Jesus told the church of Ephesus, "Remember from where you have fallen, and repent and do the deeds you did at first; or else I am coming to you and will remove your lampstand out of its place—unless you repent" (Revelation 2:5).

This statement is especially haunting when compared to what we know about the churches in Ephesus from other places in Scripture. Paul had spent several years teaching them the Word of God (cf. Acts 20). The letter he wrote to them is a treasure chest of deep theological truths that would have been given only to people who had the maturity to process such lofty ideas. Yet now they had retreated spiritually to a place where they were in need of serious self-examination.

The Lord suggested that these people should go back to their pasts to review where they had been spiritually. Such an analysis would convict them and motivate them to turn around.

For You

You will find this chapter especially relevant if you fall into "the past is everything" side of the equation. Persons in that category often think and speak about the past entirely in the negative. Because certain aspects of their past have been so painful, they see no way their past could ever be their friend.

I'm sure that many who read this book could tell horrible stories of disappointment, affliction, abuse, and suffering. I do not seek to minimize in any way the pain of those experiences. We will spend a significant amount of time in later chapters finding biblical answers for those who suffer.

However, my concern at this point is for those who, because of difficulties in the past, have closed their minds entirely to this area of their life. If that is true for you, you may not be benefitting from all the resources God has given you to grow in Him.

Review the ways God has blessed you. Rejoice in past victories.

Marvel at the sweet times of forgiveness. Be humbled by the times you have failed. Do not let the painful aspects of the past hinder you from the good that can result from cultivating this friendship.

A Grand Assumption

Thus far I have been writing as if every reader has a personal relationship with God. I realize that may or may not be true in your case. Dealing with the past requires many hard steps. There is no easy way to sort out the various nuances that may be true of anyone's past. But making progress in the right direction will be impossible without God (Hebrews 11:6).

Scripture teaches that all people are born in sin (Romans 3:23) and are therefore separated from God (Isaiah 59:2; Romans 6:23; 1 Timothy 2:5). We are also told that we cannot somehow earn our way to heaven by our good works (Ephesians 2:8-9; Titus 3:5).

The great news is that God chose to love us in spite of our condition and to demonstrate that love most supremely by sending His Son to die in our place on the cross (John 3:16; Ephesians 5:8; 2 Corinthians 5:21). The price He paid was accepted by the Father who in turn miraculously raised Jesus from the dead (1 Corinthians 15:3-4). That means that any person, regardless of his or her past, can become a child of God by repenting of his or her sin and trusting Jesus Christ as Savior and Lord (Romans 10:9-10,13).

Part of the beauty of salvation is that you can know for sure that you have received it. One of the primary verses used to draw me to Christ was 1 John 5:13: "These things I have written to you who believe in the name of the Son of God, so that you may know that you have eternal life."

Another benefit of knowing Christ is the Holy Spirit, who indwells (resides in) the heart of every Christian (1 Corinthians 6:19-20). He stands ready to teach you, lead you, fill (control) you, and develop His fruit in you.

There is also the joy, according to passages such as 1 John 2:1-2, of having Jesus seated at the right hand of God interceding for your every need. With and through Him, there is nothing about your past that you cannot overcome (Philippians 4:13).

If you are not sure that you have ever repented of your sin and believed in the finished work of Christ alone for your salvation, why not take that step right now by placing your faith and trust in Him? It will completely change your ability to handle the next stages of our journey together (2 Corinthians 5:17).

For Jill

The first few sessions with Jill were primarily devoted to listening with compassion and empathy and gathering additional data. Biblical counselors believe in following James's admonition that "everyone must be quick to hear, slow to speak and slow to anger" (1:19).

It became apparent as Jill continued to tell her story that there was more to her past than just the ways others had abused her. Yes, her suffering had been prolonged and intense. But she also began to intimate ways that she too had fallen short. There were reasons her mother had declared her to be incorrigible. Her cryptic statement on her entrance form that "she had acceptance issues" began to be filled out with details about relational tendencies that were unhealthy, to put it mildly. In multiple ways the choices Jill had made in the past were hindering her spiritually and contributing to her present emotional state.

However, we were not ready yet to begin focusing on all those things. I determined that Jill's greatest need was to understand more of *the sustaining gospel*. As I mentioned earlier, Jill believed that she had become a Christian in her younger years, and when I asked her about that, I had no reason to doubt her sincerity. But it seemed the gospel was something she believed in the past and was trusting to get her to heaven in the future. The notion that it had any relevance to her present struggles was not part of her working theology.

Jill needed to begin to think of her identity with words other than "abused" and "depressed." Both of those descriptions were true for sure. But they were not the most important things about her.

As a Christian, she was "in Christ" (Ephesians 1:3). She had been chosen before the foundation of the world (1:4) and adopted into God's family (1:5). She could rejoice that "in Him we have redemption through His blood, the forgiveness of our trespasses, according to the riches of His grace which He lavished on us" (1:7-8). We determined, with the help of God, that we would follow the example of John the Baptist, who declared of Jesus, "He must increase but I must decrease" (John 3:30). As Elyse Fitzpatrick and Dennis Johnson so helpfully explain,

> Most of us have never really understood that Christianity is not a self-help religion meant to enable moral people to become more moral. We don't need a self-help book; we need a Savior. We don't need to get our collective act together; we need death and resurrection and the life-transforming truths of the gospel. And we don't need them just once, at the beginning of our Christian life; we need them every moment of every day.[1]

Being in Christ meant that Jill could cry out to her sympathetic high priest (Hebrews 4:15) and "draw near with confidence to the throne of grace, so that we may receive mercy and find grace to help in time of need" (4:16). As the beauty and sufficiency of Jesus became more apparent (John 1:14-16), the past became a less intimidating beast (John 16:33).

Jill could also be honest about the power and presence of sin in everyone—her abusers, her counselor, and even herself (Romans 5:10-11). She could glory in the cross (1 Corinthians 1:18) and begin to "comprehend with all the saints what is the breadth and length and height and depth, and to know the love of Christ which surpasses knowledge, that you may be filled up to all the fullness of God" (Ephesians 3:18-19).

Yes, Jill had been united with Christ in His sufferings (Romans 6:3; Philippians 3:10; Colossians 3:3; 2 Corinthians 1:3-8). But as many preachers have eloquently proclaimed over the years, "that was Friday." The most glorious aspect of the sustaining gospel is that Jill was also united with her resurrected and ascended Lord (Romans 6:4-5; Philippians 3:11-14; Colossians 3:1; 2 Corinthians 1:9-10).

This meant that nothing about Jill's past had to be feared, ignored, or excused. She was *in Christ.* Now it was time to begin exploring how her resurrected Savior could begin leading her through the process of growing from her past.

Are you ready to do that as well? This same process is available to you. Yes, it requires courage and a willingness to open up your heart and life. But the sustaining gospel can give you the strength and courage you need to take the next steps in your journey.

Questions for Personal Reflection

1. Describe several challenging events where God gave you the strength and wisdom you needed to serve and please Him even when it was hard. Look for an opportunity this week consciously to view a current challenge through the lens of a past success.
2. List five to ten ways God has blessed you in days gone by. How can you be a better steward of these past blessings? Cultivate the habit of reviewing them often and having a thankful heart for what God has done. Job factored God's past blessings into the way he responded to his present trials. How would your response to problems be different if you rehearsed God's past blessings in your life?
3. How would you evaluate yourself on practicing spiritual candor? Are you honest with yourself and others about what is occurring emotionally? Can you relate to the psalmist when he said, "I pour out my soul within me" (Psalm 42:4)? What are some times when you have done that?

Questions for Group Discussion

1. Does the average Christian view the past as his or her friend? Explain your answer. How has our world's emphases in this area made it more challenging to adopt a biblical approach?
2. Ask two or three people to share about a trial they are currently facing. How would a person who remembers blessings from the past handle the trial as compared to a person who does not?
3. Ask one or more people to describe a struggle they are having in the way they respond to another person's failure or weakness. How does being rightly related to the past help develop an approach that is humble and gracious?

Chapter Four

You Can Learn to Put the Past in Its Place

When I was in Bible college, I was 700 miles away from my family. That meant that I made a lot of trips back and forth for holidays, summer breaks, and other special events. This was back in the days when the speed limit was 55 miles per hour, and a trip of that length seemed to take forever.

On one of those journeys I was riding in the front seat of a friend's car when he looked at me and said, "Let's switch drivers." I assumed he meant that we would pull off at the next exit and find a place to stop the car and exchange places. Apparently in his mind that would have taken far too much time. His proposal, which he assured me he had done many times, was to exchange places *while driving*. Being the smart yet adventurous college student I was, I readily agreed. And believe it or not, we were able to perform that trick without even slowing down.

Over time that became a common practice on cross-country trips for me, including the time my younger sister, who also attended the same college, and I were heading home for Thanksgiving break. We were right in the middle of the switch, going down a mountainside on an interstate highway, when we hit a bump. Several things happened at once, beginning with my knee hitting the steering wheel. The car then started spinning in circles, and on the third revolution, we slammed into a guardrail. Amazingly no one was hurt, but my car sustained significant damage.

A Multifaceted Problem

When I got home, I explained to my parents what had happened and placed as much blame as possible on my sister (after all, she wasn't as experienced at switching places as I was—it was obviously her fault). The problem now was that my car was a multifaceted wreck. There was the obvious damage to the body, and there were also questions about the engine, the transmission, and other components.

Resolving a multifaceted problem requires the involvement of several different skill sets. The body guy could deal with the dented fenders, but he didn't know anything about transmissions. The engine guy could check the motor, but you wouldn't want him repainting the body. A multifaceted problem requires a multifaceted solution.

Your past is multifaceted as well. I hope by now you are convinced that this area of your life is a powerful entity, for either good or ill. But some of God's people have not given this area the attention it deserves. If that description fits you, my hope is that you are now motivated to think more carefully and comprehensively about your past.

Your Past Is Not One Big Lump

Many people make the mistake of thinking about their past as if it were a large, mysterious entity that cannot be understood, classified, or properly addressed. That is not true. God's Word can help anyone handle their past well.

One of the first steps is assigning the various events of your past to the appropriate biblical categories. To do this, you must carefully answer two clarifying questions.

First, *was this an event where you **suffered** (either because another person directly sinned against you or because you faced general trials as a result of living in a sin-cursed world) or where you **sinned**?*

Let's call the first possibility *your innocent past.* In other words, it was not initiated by anything you did wrong.

We'll call the other category *your guilty past.* In these cases, at the risk of sounding like a junior high boy, you started it. It's important to see that the Word of God has answers for both situations. However, if you fail to clarify the nature of the problem, you can be certain you will fail to find and apply the appropriate solution.

Organizing the Past

In what occurred, you were…

INNOCENT	GUILTY
Occasions of suffering	Occasions of sinning

The second clarifying question is, *How did you respond?* Sometimes when we suffer or are sinned against (the innocent past), we respond properly. At other times we displease God in what we choose to think, say, or do next.

The same is true about events from our guilty past. Sometimes we sin, but then we quickly turn ourselves around. At other times we sin, and then we take additional steps down the wrong path that further displease God.

Organizing the Past

You responded…	
WELL	Your response to the event pleased God.
POORLY	Your response to the event displeased God.

The Four Options

Viewing the past in this fashion gives us four different possible categories. Think about these options as buckets, and the events from your past as Ping-Pong balls. Your task is to properly organize your past events so you are best positioned to apply the appropriate scriptural truths to each situation. Let's use the following terminology as we move forward together.

The innocent past when you responded well

As we mentioned above, the innocent past is comprised of the times when you suffered because someone sinned against you or because of trials you faced as a result of living in a sin-cursed world. On some occasions when you were sinned against, by God's grace you responded in a way that pleased the Lord. You might still feel the effects of this event (for reasons we will discuss in subsequent chapters), but you have not compounded the problem by reacting in a sinful way.

The innocent past when you responded poorly

Often being sinned against catches us off guard. We usually aren't prepared for mistreatment, injustice, or abuse. And even when we expect such treatment, it always hurts. Too frequently our response to such treatment displeases God. A harsh answer. The cold shoulder. Sarcasm. Revenge. We were not responsible for what initially happened, but we should not have responded the way we did.

God's Word has sufficient answers for each aspect of the innocent past. However, you must first assign each event from the times you suffered to the appropriate category if you ever hope to find the correct biblical principles as you seek to move forward in your relationship with God.

The guilty past when you responded well

The guilty past is made up of those occasions initiated by your own wrongdoing. The problem would have never occurred were it not for your sin. Thankfully in some cases we allow the Holy Spirit to quickly convict us of what we have done. Although our initial word or deed violated Scripture, our subsequent steps brought us closer to God and the party we offended.

The guilty past when you responded poorly

But sometimes we strike out twice. Not only did our sin initiate the conflict but our next choices made things worse. The chart below illustrates the way these categories relate to one another:

Organizing the Past

In what occurred, you were…

You responded…	INNOCENT	GUILTY
WELL	You were sinned against but you responded well.	You sinned but handled it quickly.
POORLY	You were sinned against but you responded poorly.	You sinned and responded poorly (with additional sin).

A clarifying note about the categories

It is okay if your "baloney detector" is going off right about now. I am not suggesting that the Bible teaches these four categories in some sort of absolute and rigid fashion. Rather, these categories help us to clarify what happened and how we responded. That, in turn, helps us know what biblical principles to apply. Part of the task of constructing a biblical theology on any topic is to develop categories that are admittedly man-made in an attempt to organize all that Scripture says about a given subject.

For example, consider "theology proper," the doctrine of God. Historically theologians have categorized God's attributes into various divisions, but the number of categories they choose is somewhat arbitrary because it is possible to categorize God's attributes in different ways. The categories also overlap because God's attributes are not disconnected from one another. His holiness is always loving and His love is always holy.

The point is, I am posing these four categories as one possible way to organize the events from your past. I have found this setup to be a good way to apply Scripture systematically to my own life and then, in turn, to help my counselees. If you think it is more helpful to categorize the troubling events from your past in a different way, I encourage you to adapt and improve what is written here.

The Grand Prize Game

People exposed to children's television in the 1960s (yes, we had TV back then) might recognize my bucket and Ping-Pong ball metaphor. It comes from a program called *Bozo the Clown,* which always ended, as far as I can remember, with two children lined up behind a series of buckets. Each child was given a Ping-Pong ball and instructed to toss it into Bucket One. If a child succeeded, he or she was given another Ping-Pong ball and told to try for Bucket Two. If a child got the balls in the right buckets, he or she won the game.

When it comes to your past, this is anything but a game. But I encourage you to categorize thoughtfully the events from your past that especially trouble you. We will see in subsequent chapters that God's Word can help you address each type of event. The goal is eventually to empty the buckets, and we'll discuss later in much more detail what I mean by these buckets truly being empty. But the critical first step is learning how to categorize events from your past well. Using our bucket metaphor, the chart below serves as the roadmap we'll be following:

Understanding the Buckets

In what occurred, you were…

You responded…	INNOCENT	GUILTY
WELL	BUCKET 1 The innocent past when you responded well	BUCKET 3 The guilty past when you responded well
POORLY	BUCKET 2 The innocent past when you responded poorly	BUCKET 4 The guilty past when you responded poorly

The Beauty of Narratives

Learning to think about life in an organized, biblical manner requires effort, prayer, and reliance upon the Holy Spirit of God. As we will soon discover, Scripture gives us many opportunities to see these four categories of the past in action.

A significant portion of the Bible is comprised of narratives or stories. The apostle Paul tells us that "whatever was written in earlier times was written for our instruction, so that through perseverance and the encouragement of the Scriptures we might have hope" (Romans 15:4). To help you better categorize the events from your past, let's practice by using real-life experiences from several characters in God's Word.

Bucket One: Joseph—The Innocent Past and a Right Response

The account of Joseph in Genesis 37–50 is one of the most compelling stories in all the Word of God. The amount of space devoted to Joseph's life, compared to all the other important men and women in Genesis, is instructive. There was something unique and special about the way God worked in and through Joseph. That is not to suggest that Joseph's life was easy or problem free; his days were characterized in many ways by grinding affliction.

The intensity of his suffering

Many "health and wealth" teachers today say that people who cultivate the right kind of faith can live a life free of hardship and trial. Joseph's story contradicts such a notion at practically every turn.

At the hands of his jealous brothers

Joseph was Jacob's eleventh son. Because Joseph was the first child of Jacob's favorite wife, Rachel, Jacob favored Joseph over the other sons and gave him a multicolored coat. Also, God had revealed to Joseph in a series of dreams that Joseph's brothers would all bow to him one day. As a result, the brothers were jealous and came to despise Joseph.

One day Jacob asked Joseph to check on his older brothers who were tending the family's flocks. As Joseph approached his brothers, "they plotted against him to put him to death. They said to one another, 'Here comes this dreamer! Now then, come and let us kill him and throw him into one of the pits; and we will say, "A wild beast devoured him." Then let us see what will become of his dreams!'" (37:18-20).

This passage illustrates the cruelty that resides in the heart of humanity. Not only were these men willing to murder their own brother, they had no apparent concern for how their actions would affect their father. Fortunately Joseph was "rescued" from this fate by the oldest brother, Reuben, who suggested that they not shed Joseph's blood but instead just throw him into a pit. The brothers chose this path and then "sat down to eat a meal" (37:25).

While they were enjoying their lunch (why let a little thing like planning to kill your brother get in the way of a good meal?), a band of traders went by. Judah then told the others, "'What profit is it for us to kill our brother and cover up his blood? Come and let us sell him to the Ishmaelites and not lay our hands on him, for he is our brother, our own flesh.' And his brothers listened to him" (37:26-27).

Have you ever considered how Joseph felt when he was sold into slavery by his own brothers? Imagine the degradation of being hauled out of a pit and shackled by slave traders and the feelings of shock, betrayal, loneliness, and fear.

At the hands of his wicked temptress

Joseph was taken to Egypt and sold as a slave to a man named Potiphar. Scripture says Joseph was such an excellent worker that "his master saw that the LORD was with him and how the LORD caused all that he did to prosper in his hand" (39:3). The fact that an Egyptian official like Potiphar would come to this conclusion about Yahweh, the God of Israel, speaks volumes about the way Joseph had chosen to respond to his brothers' abuses. Is there any question about which of our four buckets these events from Joseph's past should be assigned?

Because of his faithfulness, Joseph was placed in charge of Potiphar's entire household. Then while Potiphar was gone, Potiphar's wife "looked with desire at Joseph, and she said, 'Lie with me.' But he refused and said to his master's wife, 'Behold, with me here, my master does not concern himself with anything in the house, and he has put all that he owns in my charge. There is no one greater in this house than I, and he has withheld nothing from me except you, because you are his wife. How then could I do this great evil and sin against God?'" (39:6-9).

Potiphar's wife continued to pursue Joseph. Because he would not give in to her advances, she concocted a lie about Joseph attacking her. Then Potiphar had Joseph thrown in prison.

At the hands of his thankless colleagues

In prison, Joseph met two men, who each had unusual dreams. They explained their dilemma to Joseph, who then asked them, "Do not interpretations belong to God?" (40:8). Joseph accurately interpreted their dreams with this simple request: "Keep me in mind when it goes well with you, and please do me a kindness by mentioning me to Pharaoh and get me out of this house" (40:14). Amazingly, after the dreams came true just as Joseph predicted, the men forgot to honor Joseph's simple request and left him to rot in jail.

There is no indication anywhere in this story that Joseph was in any way responsible for the suffering he endured. At this time he was entirely innocent. However, the narrative was not simply about his incredible suffering.

The power and beauty of his response

Let's fast-forward to the end of the story. After a series of amazing events orchestrated by the sovereign hand of God, Joseph meets his brothers again. By now Joseph is serving as the prime minister of Egypt, having been promoted by Pharaoh to the number two position in the nation. By God's design Joseph has stockpiled a surplus of food that is now needed by people throughout the region because of an extensive famine.

Joseph's brothers did not even recognize him anymore, and when he eventually revealed himself to them, they rightly feared for their lives. Yet the same man who testified for Yahweh in Potiphar's house and in prison and in Pharaoh's court, came through again:

> "I am your brother Joseph, whom you sold into Egypt. Now do not be grieved or angry with yourselves, because you sold me here, for God sent me before you to preserve life. For the famine has been in the land these two years, and there are still five years in which there will be neither plowing nor harvesting. God sent me before you to preserve for you a remnant in the earth, and to keep you alive by a great deliverance. Now, therefore, it was not you who sent me here, but God" (Genesis 45:4-8).

Joseph very easily could have become bitter at his brothers. He could have taken the easy path with Potiphar's wife. He could have stopped believing in the power and faithfulness of God when his brothers sold him into slavery. And when the opportunity arose, he could have exacted incredibly sweet revenge.

But Joseph didn't choose any of these wrong responses because he refused to let suffering define his existence. His response to being sinned against brought great honor and glory to his God, the One who gave him the strength to follow His will and accomplish His plan.

Undoubtedly you too have experiences that fit in this first bucket. You suffered or were sinned against, but by God's grace you responded well. By allowing such events to become part of your past and responding positively, you demonstrated the power of God in ways that greatly pleased Him.

Bucket Two: Naomi—The Innocent Past and a Poor Response

We read about Naomi back in chapter 1. There is no question she also suffered. Your heart is moved when you think about the pain she must have felt when she lost not only her husband but also her two sons.

But compared to Joseph, there is a significant difference in the way she responded. Joseph was so committed to worshipping Yahweh, even in the midst of suffering, that Potiphar, his fellow prisoners, and even Pharaoh were able to witness God's power at work.

On the other hand, Naomi encouraged her daughters-in-law to return to their families and "their gods" (Ruth 1:15). She claimed that "the hand of the Lord had gone out against" her (1:13). When the women in Bethlehem asked, "Is this Naomi?" she said, "'Do not call me Naomi; call me Mara, for the Almighty has dealt very bitterly with me. I went out full, but the Lord has brought me back empty. Why do you call me Naomi, since the Lord has witnessed against me and the Almighty has afflicted me?'" (1:19-21).

Both Joseph and Naomi fit under the heading of people with "innocent pasts" because there is no biblical reason to believe that they did anything to bring on their affliction. But that is where the similarities stop. Joseph allowed God to give him the strength to handle suffering well. Naomi chose the opposite path, and the result was a bitter heart.

Bucket Three: Peter—The Guilty Past and a Right Response

The third and fourth buckets are entirely different from the first two. Now we are talking about problems initiated by a person's wrong choice. Most of us will not have to think hard to remember situations involving our own "guilty past." We made a poor choice or committed a sin, and we either responded well or didn't. It's like spilling milk on the floor. We can either wipe it up with a clean towel and make the problem go away, or we can wipe it up with a greasy rag and make the problem worse.

Consider Peter's denials of Jesus Christ. Jesus told Peter at the Last Supper that Peter would deny Him three times (Luke 22:34). However, Jesus was already looking ahead to Peter's repentance and restoration when He said, "'When you have returned to Me, strengthen your brethren'" (v. 32).

Peter's failure here is one of the best known stories in all of Scripture. After Peter denied Jesus the third time, "Immediately, while he was still speaking, a rooster crowed. The Lord turned and looked at Peter. And Peter remembered the word of the Lord, how He had told him, 'Before a rooster crows today, you will deny Me three times.' And he went out and wept bitterly" (Luke 22:60-62).

Peter's heart had already broken over the sin he had committed, and Jesus, the sovereign Lord of heaven and earth, knew it. That is why after the resurrection, Christ orchestrated a special event just for His weak but beloved disciple. It occurred after Peter and several of his friends had gone fishing all night and caught nothing. A man from the shore asked if they had any fish. When they said no, He encouraged them to cast their net on the right side of the boat (John 21:6). They did so, and were unable to draw the net back because of the great number of fish.

John then exclaimed, "It is the Lord" (v. 7). Peter, in typical Peter fashion, couldn't wait until the boat reached land. Instead he wrapped his outer garment around him and "plunged into the sea" (v. 7). The text ends with Jesus graciously allowing Peter to affirm his love for His Savior three times, matching the number of times he had denied Him.

Because Peter dealt with his sin quickly, he was able to focus immediately on the job Jesus had for him. He listened to the Great Commission (Matthew 28:19-20) and became a great leader in the early church.

Yes, Peter's denials were a significant lapse of faith. But by repenting and seeking restoration right away, he prevented his failure from sidetracking his life and ministry.

What sets this third bucket apart from the others and why is it important? Some people fail, ask forgiveness, and then continue to beat themselves up for what they did. They replay the event over and over. They question whether God has truly forgiven them. Worried about who might find out about their failures, they avoid opportunities to get to know other people or to serve in their church.

Peter didn't do any of those things. Once his failure was behind him, he accepted Christ's forgiveness and moved on. Though he was guilty and responsible for his poor choices, he responded well.

Bucket Four: David—The Guilty Past and a Wrong Response

Regrettably, we all have also had times when we sinned, and then we compounded the problem by responding with additional thoughts, words, or actions that displeased God.

That point would not be hard to prove from King David's life, would it? One name immediately brings a specific story to mind: Bathsheba. Because this is a familiar story to most, and because I will return to it again in chapter 12, I will give only a brief summary here. You can read the account for yourself in 2 Samuel 11.

On a sultry evening King David walked out onto his rooftop and saw on another rooftop the wife of one of his generals bathing. It would have been wonderful if David had shielded his eyes and cried out to God for protection from this temptation. Instead, David sent for her, had sex with her, and she became pregnant.

Unfortunately, David dealt with his guilt by trying to cover his tracks. He brought Bathsheba's husband, Uriah, home from battle, assuming he and Bathsheba would enjoy sexual relations as husband and wife, and the "problem" of Bathsheba's pregnancy would be covered up. When that ploy failed, David sent Uriah back to the battlefront and arranged with his commander, Joab, to position Uriah in the worst part of the battle so he would be killed. Then David brought Bathsheba to his house, and she became his wife. Lest there be any doubt that David responded poorly to his original bad decision, the writer of 2 Samuel concludes chapter 11 with these ominous words: "But the thing that David had done was evil in the sight of the LORD" (11:27).

As horrible as David's adultery was, his subsequent choices greatly compounded the problem. Rather than deal with his sin, David allowed his unconfessed actions to become part of his past. Some might argue, "But didn't David eventually repent?" Yes, by God's grace, he did. However, had David repented immediately, Uriah would have still been alive, among other things. By refusing to repent and by making additional wrong choices, David significantly worsened his situation.

What About You?

Do you also have events from your guilty past that have yet to be fully addressed? What reasons have you given for not dealing with these events in a way that would honor God and put the matter to rest? What other wrong choices have you made to cover your initial actions? How have these unaddressed matters affected you? In what ways are they still affecting you?

If you find yourself in this condition, I encourage you to read carefully two psalms David wrote when he was in this very situation, Psalms 38 and 51. Many of the verses may sound as if David has been reading your mail. But the passages are also filled with hope and joy because they affirm you don't have to live in the fourth bucket forever.

Hope for Jill

As Jill became more comfortable with the implications of the sustaining gospel, she was much more open to discussing her past. There was no longer doubt in anyone's mind, especially hers, that there was a direct connection between the debilitating depression she had experienced for so many years and the significant amount of unfinished business she had with the past.

What gave Jill great hope was learning that there was a way to categorize the problems in her life and then deal with each category using principles from God's Word. I am not saying that her story quickly and easily became a neat, tidy package. It was a messy process filled with zigs and zags. But Jill was beginning to use Scripture as her guide to organize her life. She knew she wasn't responsible for everything that had occurred in her past. She recognized that the times she had agreed with those who said everything was her fault had sent her into a tailspin.

But choosing to ignore it all had not been helpful either. Jill wanted to know, and needed to know, what "biblical sufferology" looked like. How could she go from being like Naomi to being like Joseph? The thought that this was even possible gave her great hope.

Jill was also becoming convinced that those who encouraged her to position herself simply as a passive victim were not helping either. Because of her growing confidence in the finished work of Christ on her behalf, she was more open to considering how some of her past problems had been initiated by her own choices. But what was she supposed to do with all of that? Could she really go from being like David who made wrong choices after his sin with Bathsheba to Peter who handled his denials rapidly?

Jill knew she wasn't responsible for everything wrong in her life. But she was responsible for some things. It was time to bring out the buckets and help her sort, and then properly address, the events from her past that needed addressing.

Questions for Personal Reflection

1. List two or three of the most significant ways people have sinned against you. Who were they? What did they do? How did you respond? What is your relationship like with them today? Do you ever think about these events now?
2. List two or three of the most significant ways you have sinned in the past. What are the skeletons in your closet? How did you handle each event after it occurred? How did it affect your life in subsequent days? How do you typically respond

after you have sinned? How significant a part of your past have events like these become?

3. Do you have any unresolved sins against God or others? Take a few moments and jot down the names of the people involved, and describe what caused the breach in your relationship. How frequently do you think about this situation? Does it ever affect the way you relate to other people today? Do you experience guilt as a result? Do you have thoughts similar to those expressed by David in Psalm 38?

Questions for Group Discussion

1. What are some typical ways people are sinned against? How does the average person handle such occasions? Once the typical responses become part of a person's past, what are some of the possible long-term effects?
2. Was David's reaction to his sin with Bathsheba typical in any way? How does this dynamic play itself out in the common sins men and women commit every day? What is the price of not handling your guilty past in a more godly and biblical way? What impact could your guilty past have on present relationships?
3. What is your response to Jill's story thus far? Are there people in the typical church who struggle in similar ways? How does the typical church respond to such a person? How does the secular world respond to someone like Jill?

Section Two

Dealing with the Hurts of the Innocent Past

Chapter Five

Bad Things Happen to Good People: Another Look

We have seen that the Word of God has much to say about the topic of the past. And when God addresses something, He addresses it well. That should immediately give us hope when it comes to dealing with our pasts.

Where We've Been

As we move forward in our pursuit to handle our pasts in a biblical and God-honoring way, let's briefly review some key points that will remind us how we can best view this area of our lives.

The past is everything?

Back in chapter 1 we observed that many people in our culture believe that the past is everything. They routinely absolve themselves from choices today by hearkening back to something that occurred in days gone by. While we always want to "weep with those who weep" (Romans 12:15) and "put on a heart of compassion" (Colossians 3:12), there are two problems with the perspective that the past is everything. First, the past is viewed almost exclusively in negative ways. Second, the possible ways an individual may have sinned in response to past mistreatment is seldom considered.

Those who fall into this extreme can learn from Scripture that the past can be one of our greatest friends. God deliberately made us with the capacity to remember. Failing to benefit from this in all the ways God intended is to jettison a significant tool for spiritual growth and development.

The past is nothing?

Others believe that the past is nothing. They are quick to speak about behavioral responsibilities, the duties and disciplines of the Christian life, and gospel imperatives (what Christians should *do*) as opposed to gospel indicatives (who Christians *are*). Their lives are often characterized by activity, busyness, and at times a self-righteously critical view of those who do not measure up to their pace.

I have observed over the years that such persons often run out of behavioral steam. That is because the past can be one of our worst enemies. Trying to act properly on the outside without addressing issues of the heart is like trying to drive a car faster when the check engine light is flashing. The Bible is rife with examples of men and women who ignored the past in ways that eventually took its toll. The wheels of God's justice grind slowly, but they grind oh so fine.

One big lump?

Yet another major hindrance to finding biblical balance on the past is failing to think as precisely about it as God's Word would lead us to do. In many areas of the Christian life we tend to think in ways that are fuzzy and therefore unprofitable. That's why the discipline of building a clear biblical theology or perspective is such an important exercise.

Regarding the past, too many of us frequently think about our past as if it were all one big lump. Scripture calls us to something better that helps us organize past events into four distinct categories. But first, we need to ask two clarifying questions about those events:

1. Are we talking about your *innocent past* (times when you were sinned against directly or suffered as the result of living in a sin-cursed world) or your *guilty past* (times when you initiated the problem by your own wrong choices)?
2. How did you respond once the event occurred?

Dividing the past into four categories

In chapter 4 the answers to those two questions led to the creation of four mental buckets in which to assign past events that still may be troubling us today:

1. *The innocent past when you responded well* describes those times when you were sinned against, but by God's grace, you did not sin in return.
2. *The innocent past when you responded poorly* refers to times when you were sinned against (and it wasn't your fault), but your response displeased God (which *was* your fault).
3. *The guilty past when you responded well* speaks of times when you blew it, but then quickly acknowledged your failure and handled it appropriately before things became any worse.
4. *The guilty past when you responded poorly* describes situations in which you sinned and then took additional steps that displeased God further.

Understanding the Buckets

In what occurred, you were...

You responded...	INNOCENT	GUILTY
WELL	BUCKET 1 The innocent past when you responded well	BUCKET 3 The guilty past when you responded well
POORLY	BUCKET 2 The innocent past when you responded poorly	BUCKET 4 The guilty past when you responded poorly

In all four scenarios, Scripture provides principles that can help us learn and grow from our past. But it's essential that we properly understand each category and the scriptural principles that relate to it. Otherwise, we might end up misapplying Scripture or assuming we have resolved a past issue when that is not really the case.

Where We're Going

It's time to begin reaching into the buckets. This next section of the book will examine buckets 1 and 2, the two aspects of our innocent past. As we move into this section, I do so with a bit of fear and trembling. I have often thought about and prayed for those who read this book. It could be a person who was sexually abused as a child. Or it could be a woman whose ex-husband was a saint on Sunday and an adulterer the rest of the week. It might be a man whose retirement funds were wiped out by an unscrupulous company executive. The list is practically endless of the despicable ways people have been treated in their past, through no fault of their own.

So as I continue writing, I hope that I can somehow offer counsel from God's Word that brings comfort, healing, and hope. While I do not know what you have experienced in your past, God does, and in His Word you will find the help you need.

Each of us will have to decide what place the Bible should have in this process. The point of this chapter is to help us consider what could happen if God's Word is not given the position of authority it deserves.

A Sobering Story

Perhaps you are familiar with the book *When Bad Things Happen to Good People* by Rabbi Harold Kushner. First published in 1981, this volume has sold over four million copies to date. It was on *The New York Times* bestsellers list for months, and we can safely assume that many people in our culture have been influenced by Kushner's view.

Horrible news

One of the attractive elements of this book is that it is not written by a cold theologian or a calloused academician. Harold Kushner wrote because he and his wife had a son named Aaron who suffered from progeria, also known as rapid aging. The Kushners were told when Aaron was three years old that he would "never grow much beyond three feet in height, would have no hair on his head or body, would look like a little old man while he was still a child, and would die in his early teens."[1]

On a personal note

When I read those words, I immediately thought of the day my wife, Kris, and I received a call from our doctor to report on the tests a pediatric ophthalmologist had recently run on our newly adopted son, Andrew. He was just four weeks old, and we already knew he had suffered a serious abnormality early in his development, probably before his birth mother even knew she was pregnant. As a result, he had multiple neurological problems and a severely underdeveloped pituitary gland that would require hormone treatments each day to preserve his life. The doctors also suspected that Andrew would have significant developmental delays and be at risk for a host of other medical problems.

The pediatric ophthalmologist had been consulted because children with this cluster of symptoms often struggle with some form of blindness. Initially we shrugged this off as the doctors giving the worst-case scenario (he had looked at us, hadn't he?). Besides, we were thankful that we had a diagnosis and treatment plan that would at least preserve Andrew's life. Then we received the ophthalmologist's report, which included phrases such as "the smallest optic nerves he's ever seen" and "probably totally blind" and "we're so sorry."

Because of this, my initial response to Kushner is that of a fellow traveler who can to some degree relate to what the Kushner family must have experienced emotionally, mentally, and spiritually the day they received the prognosis for their son.

Whose Fault?

Rabbi Kushner explains the way he initially processed the news about his son:

> What I mostly felt that day was a deep, aching sense of unfairness. It didn't make sense. I had been a good person. I had tried to do what was right in the sight of God. More than that, I was living a more religiously committed life than most people I knew, people who had large, healthy families. I believed that I was following God's ways and doing His work. How could this be happening to my family? If God existed, if He was minimally fair, let alone loving and forgiving, how could He do this to me?...
>
> Like most people, my wife and I had grown up with an image of God as an all-wise, all-powerful parent figure who would treat us as our earthly parents did, or even better. If we were obedient and deserving, He would reward us. If we got out of line, He would discipline us, reluctantly but firmly. He would protect us from being hurt or from hurting ourselves, and would see to it that we got what we deserved in life.[2]

You cannot help but weep for a young rabbi and his family during a time of such unexpected and painful suffering. There is also nothing inherently wrong with expressing his honest questions about the character of God in light of what he was experiencing. Back in chapter 2 we saw the prophet Habakkuk do the same, and we will discuss more fully the process of crying out to God as we continue to address suffering in the midst of an innocent past.

However, the rabbi's questions must not simply be respectfully and compassionately heard; they should also be carefully evaluated. Is there always a direct cause/effect relationship between the way people live and the circumstances they experience? Does Scripture teach that godly living protects us from painful trials? Should people who are suffering assume that God is allowing this because of some sin in their life?

The answers to these questions can have a profound impact on the way a person handles the events we have labeled "the innocent past." Is *fairness,* by whatever measure the sufferer uses, the ultimate issue?

Turning to God's Word?

Most people would assume that a rabbi would turn eventually to God's Word for answers to these difficult and heart-wrenching questions. That is what Kushner does...sort of. He refers to Psalm 92, a marvelous text that has been a source of comfort and direction for God's people for centuries:

> It is good to give thanks to the LORD
> And to sing praises to Your name, O Most High;
> To declare Your lovingkindness in the morning
> And Your faithfulness by night,
> With the ten-stringed lute and with the harp,
> With resounding music upon the lyre.
> For You, O LORD, have made me glad by what
>   You have done,
> I will sing for joy at the works of Your hands.
> How great are Your works, O LORD!
> Your thoughts are very deep...

> The righteous man will flourish like the palm tree,
> He will grow like a cedar in Lebanon.
> Planted in the house of the Lord,
> They will flourish in the courts of our God.
> They will still yield fruit in old age;
> They shall be full of sap and very green,
> To declare that the Lord is upright;
> He is my rock, and there is no unrighteousness
> in Him.
>
> (Psalm 92:1-5,12-15)

As a pastor I have shared this psalm on numerous occasions with men and women who were suffering. I can even remember elderly persons in their final stages of life on earth who would laugh out loud when we got to the part about being "full of sap and very green." They would say things like, "That's me, pastor, full of sap," with a twinkle in their eye that comes only from many years of walking with God. The point is clear in the psalm: Because of the character and works of our faithful God, it is possible to have a joyful and worshipful heart and life even in the midst of extreme challenges.

However, when Rabbi Kushner discusses this passage, he says,

> If I could meet the author of the Ninety-second Psalm, I would first congratulate him on having composed a masterpiece of devotional literature...But having said that, I would be obliged to point out that there is a lot of wishful thinking in his theology...I find that I cannot share the optimism of the Psalmist that the righteous, in the long run, will flourish like the palm tree and give testimony to God's uprightness.[3]

I suppose we should commend Rabbi Kushner for his honesty. There is no question about his view of Scripture. And keep in mind, these words were not spoken just after receiving the diagnosis about his son, but over a decade later when he sat down to write the book.

Like many other men and women, he begins with his interpretation of his experience and then judges God and His Word through that grid. Anything that does not fit his interpretation is rejected. Saying that he "cannot share the optimism of the Psalmist" takes a fair amount of cheek, indeed.

The Proposed Solution

Students of Scripture would be quick to ask the rabbi, "But what about Job?" Kushner has an answer for that question. He devotes an entire chapter to an interpretation of Job that forms the core of the position he takes in the rest of his book.

Job was not real?

Kushner suggests that when you read the book of Job, "you realize at once that you are not reading about a real life person. This is a 'once-upon-a-time' story about a good man who suffered."[4] Kushner then summarizes his position on Job:

> To try to understand the book and its answer, let us take note of three statements which everyone in the book, and most of its readers, would like to be able to believe:
>
> A. God is all powerful and causes everything that happens in the world. Nothing happens without His willing it.
>
> B. God is just and fair, and stands for people getting what they deserve, so that the good prosper and the wicked are punished.
>
> C. Job is a good person.
>
> As long as Job is healthy and wealthy, we can believe all three of those statements at the same time with no difficulty. When Job suffers, when he loses his possessions, his family and his health, we have a problem. We can no longer make sense of all three propositions together. We can now affirm any two by denying the third.[5]

God is not powerful?

So which proposition does Rabbi Kushner advise fellow sufferers to abandon? Take a deep breath and then listen to his answer:

> Let me suggest that the author of the book of Job takes the position which neither Job nor his friends take. He believes in God's goodness and Job's goodness, and is prepared to give up his belief...that God is all powerful. Bad things do happen to good people in this world, but it is not God who wills it. God would like people to get what they deserve in life, but He cannot always arrange it. Forced to choose between a good God who is not totally powerful, or a powerful God who is not totally good, the author of the book of Job chose to believe in God's goodness.[6]

After picking themselves up off the floor, many who have studied Job would then ask the rabbi to explain God's response to Job near the end of the book:

> "Now gird up your loins like a man;
> I will ask you, and you instruct Me.
> Will you really annul My judgment?
> Will you condemn Me that you may be justified?
> Or do you have an arm like God,
> And can you thunder with a voice like His?
> Adorn yourself with eminence and dignity,
> And clothe yourself with honor and majesty.
> Pour out the overflowings of your anger,
> And look on everyone who is proud, and
> make him low.
> Look on everyone who is proud, and humble him,
> And tread down the wicked where they stand.
> Hide them in the dust together;
> Bind them in the hidden place.
> Then I will also confess to you,
> That your own right hand can save you."
> (Job 40:7-14)

You try being God?

Few places in Scripture contain a more majestic declaration of the omnipotence (all-powerful nature) of God. The clear argument of Job 40:7-14 stands in direct contrast to the position Kushner advocates. The rabbi's explanation of this apparent contradiction is:

> I take these lines to mean "if you think it is so easy to keep the world straight and true, to keep unfair things from happening to people, *you* try it." God wants the righteous to live peaceful, happy lives, but sometimes even He can't bring that about. It is too difficult even for God to keep cruelty and chaos from claiming their innocent victims. But could man, without God, do better?[7]

Can you imagine the God of heaven and earth feebly looking at a suffering human being and meekly saying, "If you think it is so easy to keep the world straight...you try it"? Such words border on blasphemy. They certainly do not reflect the character and attributes of the God of the Bible. In addition to missing the point of God's words to Job, which is that God clearly possesses power, authority, wisdom, and might, Kushner's view also fails to account for Job's response:

> Then Job answered the LORD and said,
> "I know that You can do all things,
> And that no purpose of Yours can be thwarted.
> 'Who is this that hides counsel without knowledge?'
> Therefore I have declared that which I did not
> understand,
> Things too wonderful for me, which I did not know."
> 'Hear, now, and I will speak;
> I will ask You, and You instruct me.'
> "I have heard of You by the hearing of the ear;
> But now my eye sees You;
> Therefore I retract,
> And I repent in dust and ashes."
>
> (Job 42:1-6)

A hopeless summary

Contrast Job's words with the summary Kushner gives at the end of his book:

> I believe in God. But I do not believe the same things about Him that I did years ago, when I was growing up or when I was a theology student. I recognize His limitations. He is limited in what He can do by laws of nature and by the evolution of human nature and human moral freedom. I no longer hold God responsible for illnesses, accidents, and natural disasters, because I realize that I gain little and I lose so much when I blame God for these things. I can worship a God who hates suffering but cannot eliminate it more easily than I can worship a God who chooses to make children suffer and die, for whatever exalted reason.[8]

A Point of Decision

Rabbi Kushner's story saddens me. He also makes statements that need to be addressed later in this book. But with as much grace and gentleness as I can muster, Kushner's view of Scripture is patently false. His position makes it harder for people to handle trials and suffering, not easier. One of my greatest concerns is for the millions of people who have read Kushner's book and presumably adopted its message.

My next concern is for you who are reading my book. We have come to a critical point in our journey. You must decide what you believe about the authority and sufficiency of God's Word.

It is beyond our scope to develop a comprehensive treatment of the doctrine of Scripture (which goes by the fancy name *bibliology*). I often encourage people to read James MacDonald's helpful volume *God Wrote a Book* for an understandable and relatively brief explanation of reasons to believe and trust God's Word. There are many other good books on this subject as well. But let's look to Scripture and see what it says about itself:

> "The law of the LORD is perfect, restoring the soul; The testimony of the LORD is sure, making wise the simple" (Psalm 19:7).

David says that God's Word is flawless. It has the capacity to transform the inner man (soul) and make us wise.

> "Forever, O LORD, Your word is settled in heaven" (Psalm 119:89).

The Bible is God's completed revelation to man. It is firmly fixed and therefore cannot and should not be changed.

> "'Sanctify them in the truth; Your word is truth'" (John 17:17).

Jesus prayed to His Father and asked that those who followed Him as Lord and Savior would be changed (sanctified) through the truth of God's Word.

> "All Scripture is inspired by God and profitable for teaching, for reproof, for correction, for training in righteousness; so that the man of God may be adequate, equipped for every good work" (2 Timothy 3:16-17).

The Bible is literally "breathed out" (inspired) by God to His people. It is therefore profitable and able to equip us for every good work.

> "But know this first of all, that no prophecy of Scripture is a matter of one's own interpretation, for no prophecy was ever made by an act of human will, but men moved by the Holy Spirit spoke from God" (2 Peter 1:20-21).

The Bible is a divine book. The Author is the Holy Spirit, and the process by which it was written was supernatural, unlike any other book on earth.

> "[S]eeing that His divine power has granted to us everything pertaining to life and godliness, through the true

> knowledge of Him who called us by His own glory and excellence. For by these He has granted to us His precious and magnificent promises, so that by them you may become partakers of the divine nature, having escaped the corruption that is in the world by lust" (2 Peter 1:3-4).

God has given us a book that is sufficient. Everything we need to know about how to handle the past is contained in the pages of Scripture.

These verses of Scripture can fill our hearts with hope. God has fully equipped us to face the challenges of yesterday, today, and tomorrow. His Word should be one of our greatest treasures. No wonder the psalmist said, "Your word is a lamp to my feet and a light to my path" (Psalm 119:105). Thus God's sufficient Word is always also His profoundly relevant Word—written to real people with real problems and providing real direction for real life.

To what source of truth will you turn?

Before you can utilize any of the four buckets we've discussed, you have to make a decision. What source of truth will you use to guide the way you think about your past?

The temptation to choose the wrong interpretative grid is just that—a temptation. That was the core of Satan's temptation of Adam and Eve in the garden: "has God said?" (Genesis 3:1). Are you going to trust what a person has said? Or are you going to trust what God has said?

Choose carefully

Keep in mind that the apostle Paul warned New Testament believers with these solemn words: "I am afraid that, as the serpent deceived Eve by his craftiness, your minds will be led astray from the simplicity and purity of devotion to Christ" (2 Corinthians 11:3).

Our adversary would be delighted if a person today denied God's Word as the means to interpret and properly resolve the events of the past. Thankfully, we have the model of the Second Adam, the Lord Jesus Christ, who overcame Satan's temptations in the wilderness by addressing each attack with a response directly from the Word of God. The Bible was sufficient to address whatever temptation or problem Jesus faced (Matthew 4:1-11).

Perhaps you have never thought about viewing the troubling events of your past through the lens of God's Word. To do so is literally to follow Christ. Why not pause and ask God to give you the strength and the wisdom to apply Scripture to your past?

So How Is Andrew?

As of this writing, Kris and I have had the privilege of raising our son Andrew for the past 17 years. By all accounts it appears that he will never be able to live on his own, so our plan is to continue to care for him as long as we are healthy enough to do so and as long as we are convinced that is the best option for him.

I am in no position to judge whether having a special needs child who dies as a teenager is better or worse than having a special needs child who will live with us for the rest of our life on earth. But both Kris and I can say that our personal relationship with God and faith in His Word have been sufficient sources of sustaining grace every day. Because God's Word is our guide, our challenges with Andrew are not drudgery.

Just last night I came in from doing some work outside, and Kris and Andrew were sitting in the living room reading a book together, laughing and enjoying each other's company. Yesterday while I was in the office I heard a loud roar of laughter from several fellow staff members. When I checked on what was happening, I found that Andrew, who loves bears, had just told our office staff one of his famous jokes. ("What did the bear eat after the dentist fixed his tooth? He ate the dentist.")

I believe one of the reasons Andrew can enjoy life even as a special needs child is that Kris has cared for him with the joy and grace that comes only from believing God's Word. I regularly, practically daily, hear them laughing out loud about something that has occurred.

I do not write this to minimize the depth of suffering that you may have experienced or even to ignore the challenges we face as a family. But the power of God's Word to help us handle and deal with past events and circumstances should never be minimized. As Paul told the church in Rome, "Now may the God of hope fill you with all joy and peace in believing, so that you will abound in hope by the power of the Holy Spirit" (Romans 15:13).

My hope and prayer is that every reader will choose to interpret the events of his or her past through the lens of Scripture. God has graciously provided sufficient truth so that past difficulties do not have to drag us down today. We can live victoriously regardless of what has happened to us.

However, we must decide what color glasses we will wear as we think about the events of the past. The Bible can help us see things as God does, with divine clarity and insight, if we choose to view life His way. The Lord has even said if we lack the ability to apply scriptural principles to the past, He will give us wisdom if we simply acknowledge our need and sincerely request His help (James 1:5). If you have never asked God to help you view your past in a biblical way, I strongly encourage you to do so now.

An Important Starting Point for Jill

Jill had many things in her life that were deeply disturbing. When she first came for counseling, her eyes and words were filled with fear of the oncoming winter. The depression that had enveloped her so many times before felt like a crouching lion, ready to devour her.

But Jill had several things going for her, including a strong desire to hear what God's Word said. She had tried dozens of secular approaches. Deep down she believed, or at least hoped, that the Word of God had a way of interpreting her situation that she had not yet considered. She was like those Jesus described in his Sermon on the Mount, "Blessed are those who hunger and thirst for righteousness, for they shall be satisfied" (Matthew 5:6). That hunger served her well in the days that were to come.

Questions for Personal Reflection

1. What do you believe about the authority, sufficiency, and relevancy of Scripture? How does this affect the way you handle suffering?
2. Should human beings want a God who is simply fair? Why or why not?
3. Do you believe God is all-powerful? Why or why not? What should a Christian do when what they are experiencing does not seem to match what God's Word says about His nature?

Questions for Group Discussion

1. How did various members of the group respond to Rabbi Kushner's statement that he would tell the author of Psalm 92 that he "did not share his optimism"?
2. What is the doctrine of the sufficiency of Scripture? How would you explain it to a 10-year-old in your Sunday school class?
3. In what ways do sufferers who *do* believe in the sufficiency of Scripture differ from sufferers who *do not?* In what ways are they alike?

Chapter Six

Authentic Suffering: Reaching into Bucket One

MOST OF US LIKE IT WHEN people practice full disclosure. Especially if we are considering a purchase or contemplating a new idea, we do not want to discover surprises buried in the fine print. Up-front honesty is always best.

Jesus Christ practiced full disclosure. When explaining to his disciples what it would be like to follow Him, our Lord made this startling statement: "In the world you will have tribulation" (John 16:33 ESV). That is up-front honesty. Followers of Christ will suffer.

I imagine that many who read this book could tell sobering and heartbreaking stories of the tribulation they have faced. Perhaps you are facing significant affliction right now. And the Bible is filled with examples of violence, wickedness, and unspeakable abuse. Wherever you look, people suffer.

Suffering in the Church

One weekend during the time I was writing this chapter, I was out of town participating in a training conference. About 2:00 Saturday morning, my cell phone rang. My wife, Kris, was calling to tell me that a young mother from our church and her two small children had been killed in a tragic house fire. The husband had been injured trying to save his family and was the lone survivor. As soon as possible I caught a plane home so that I could attempt to minister to this grieving husband and father.

The memorial service was held in our church sanctuary. Because of the condition of the bodies and the ages of the children, the decision was made to bury them in one large casket. I had never seen such a casket before, and I would be glad to never see another one.

When we arrived at the graveside, there was a canopy, some chairs, and a few shovels next to the freshly dug grave. After I concluded my portion of the service, the casket was lowered into the ground. Then the husband and father stood up, took one of the shovels, and began to shovel dirt around the casket. After a few moments his father and father-in-law joined him. A minute or two later, other men from the group stepped up and relieved the first men of their shovels and continued the task. At some point a person in the crowd began singing a hymn, and eventually everyone joined in. When the service was over, many stayed to hug, cry, grieve, and even rejoice.

It was a stark reminder of the implications of Jesus' words in John 16:33—people suffer.

Suffering in the Community

Our community-based counseling ministry is open to anyone from our town who would like to talk to someone. Often they tell stories of significant suffering. Men and women tell of spouses who have broken their marriage vows. Parents pour out their hearts over children who have gone astray. People speak of being mistreated at their jobs. Children tell us their parents are strung out on drugs or alcohol, and there is no responsible adult in the home. We buy tissues by the case because there is a lot of weeping.

Steps to Finding Hope

But thankfully, the stories do not have to end there. God's Word is filled with hope and help for us as we suffer. Paul was able to encourage his brothers and sisters in Rome when he said, "May the God of hope fill you with all joy and peace in believing, so that you will abound in hope by the power of the Holy Spirit" (Romans 15:13).

Isn't it wonderful that one of the ways God refers to Himself in Scripture is with the delightful phrase "the God of hope"? My prayer for every suffering person who reads this book is that you will take steps toward being filled "with all joy and peace in believing."

When I talk about Bucket One, which holds events from the innocent past to which you responded well, I am not suggesting that you should relive those hurts over and over. God wants us to put such events behind us. But to do so, you must learn to practice *authentic suffering.*

Understanding the Buckets

In what occurred, you were...

You responded...	INNOCENT	GUILTY
WELL	BUCKET 1 The innocent past when you responded well requires: **Authentic Suffering**	
POORLY		

Many passages in God's Word are tailored to men and women who have been sinned against or who are suffering because of the natural and painful effects of living in a sin-cursed world. Two especially helpful Bible passages are Psalm 73 and 2 Corinthians 1. These precious texts allow us to hear what authentic suffering sounds like and feels like, and what those who suffer wrestle with and hope for. If you have not read these passages recently, I encourage you to take a few moments to do so before proceeding with this chapter.

In the principles that follow, you won't find a step-by-step process or cookie-cutter approach to dealing with suffering. Rather, these principles can help you determine whether there are still events from your past where you have not suffered in a way that is consistent with Scripture.

Face it honestly

One of the primary reasons some events from the past are still in Bucket One is that the person who was hurt has believed ideas such as *big boys don't cry, time heals all wounds,* or *tough guys just rub dirt on it.* In our culture, we are taught a myriad of ways to ignore or deny the pain that comes from grinding affliction. However, the Word of God teaches and illustrates a dramatically different approach, often through the stories and expressions of real men and women who are open and honest about what is occurring to them, in them, and around them.

Acknowledge the confusion and hurt

Asaph, the writer of Psalm 73, is very open about how difficult and perplexing he finds his life to be. "But as for me, my feet came close to stumbling, my steps had almost slipped" (v. 2). The apostle Paul speaks in a similar way in 2 Corinthians 1 as he told his brothers and sisters in Christ about "all our affliction" (v. 4), how "the sufferings of Christ are ours in abundance" (v. 5), how "we were burdened excessively" (v. 8), and even had "the sentence of death within ourselves" (v. 9).

This approach is refreshingly different from the glib answers and plastic smiles that too often adorn the people of God. I am not suggesting that we should languish endlessly in our suffering. But both Asaph and Paul model an approach to hard times that more of us should be willing to follow—that is, to openly acknowledge the confusion and hurt suffering brings.

Love God enough to cry out to Him

Asaph leaves no doubt as to why his steps had almost slipped. He admits that he was "envious of the arrogant" and troubled by "the prosperity of the wicked" (v. 3). After a long list of what sounds dangerously close to being complaints to God, he summarizes his concerns by saying, "When I pondered to understand this, it was troublesome in my sight" (v. 16).

This is similar to what we saw back in chapter 1 about Paul's handling of his thorn in the flesh. His testimony was, "Concerning this I implored the Lord three times that it might leave me" (2 Corinthians 12:8). We often think of Paul as a hardy man who accomplished marvelous things for God. That is true. But it is equally true that Paul was man enough to cry out to God when he did not understand or appreciate what was happening in his life.

The Word of God is filled with examples of men and women who faced their hurts honestly. One of my favorite passages in the Psalms says,

> Hear my cry, O God;
> Give heed to my prayer.
> From the end of the earth I call to You when
> my heart is faint;
> Lead me to the rock that is higher than I.
> For You have been a refuge for me,
> A tower of strength against the enemy.
> Let me dwell in Your tent forever;
> Let me take refuge in the shelter of Your wings.
> (Psalm 61:1-4)

We who are followers of Christ are invited and even commanded to bring our hurts to Him. Because He is a high priest who can sympathize with our weaknesses (Hebrews 4:15), the implication is clear: "Therefore let us draw near with confidence to the throne of grace, so that we may receive mercy and find grace to help in time of need" (v. 16). We can be sure that when we love God enough to cry out to Him, we will find Him seated on "the throne of grace." Only in God can we find authority and mercy perfectly blended. Why would we ignore or deny our hurts when we have such a Savior as that?

Ask others to help

Authentic sufferers are also willing to cry out to others. There are few things worse than suffering alone. An independent spirit coupled with a phony façade is a sure-fire guarantee that events will stay in Bucket One far longer than necessary. Solomon was right when he said, "Two are better than one because they have a good return for their labor. For if either of them falls, the one will lift up his companion. But woe to the one who falls when there is not another to lift him up...A cord of three strands is not quickly torn apart" (Ecclesiastes 4:9-12).

We who are part of the church of Jesus Christ have the privilege to "bear one another's burdens, and thereby fulfill the law of Christ" (Galatians 6:2). We are called upon to "rejoice with those who rejoice, and weep with those who weep" (Romans 12:15). Some of my most treasured memories as a pastor are times when people from our church family wept and hugged and grieved together. God's Word is true—a cord of three strands is not quickly torn apart.

How about you?

Have you been honest about the hard times you faced in the past? Have you acknowledged the depth of the pain and disappointment? Have you laid out your questions before God and man? Have you cried out to the Lord in a way that is real and heartfelt? And have you surrounded yourself with spiritual friends who can help you understand your situation in light of God's Word and the abundant resources that are yours in Christ?

If you can say yes to those questions, then in your case, Bucket One is probably empty. Praise the Lord that He has allowed you to get to this place. When it comes to the past, empty buckets are a good thing.

Can Bucket One ever truly be empty?

You might wonder what I mean when I use the word *empty* in our discussion. That is an important question. I am not suggesting that your life will ever be empty of pain or sorrow. That will not occur until we get to heaven. Nor am I saying that some of the painful emotions you've experienced in life will disappear completely.

Bucket One is empty if you have taken the steps God wants you to take to process what has occurred. When you can say, "By God's grace, I have handled that," you are well on your way to growing from your past.

However, if you have unfinished business, please remember that while events do not have to stay in Bucket One forever, they will not simply jump out on their own. Psalm 73 and 2 Corinthians 1 as well as other passages are in the Bible to help us develop habits of authentic suffering. Time will not heal all wounds. Facing our suffering honestly will.

Face it biblically

A critical transition in Psalm 73 occurs in verse 17: "Until I came into the sanctuary of God..." Talk that is not tethered to a reliable source of truth is often unproductive and sometimes even damaging.

Earlier we looked at Romans 15:13, which affirms it is possible for people like you and me to abound in hope. That verse cannot be fully understood apart from what Paul explained earlier in the passage: "Whatever was written in earlier times was written for our instruction, so that through perseverance and the encouragement of the Scriptures we might have hope" (v. 4). Being willing to face our hurts honestly is part of the process that often leads us to ask questions of God's Word we would never have considered before. As outlandish as this may seem, especially if you are in the middle of suffering in your life right now, the psalmist came to the place where he could say to God, "It is good for me that I was afflicted, that I may learn Your statutes" (119:71).

This is not intended in any way to minimize the intensity of the suffering that many of God's people experience. As author Dustin Shramek has written:

> Good theology is essential if we are going to suffer well. It will help us persevere during our trials, and it will give us

> hope. We believe that "weeping may tarry for the night, but joy comes with the morning" (Psalms 30:5). It is faith in our good and sovereign God that enables us to wait until the morning. But we must never forget that often the night is long and the weeping uncontrollable.[1]

Recognize that pain and suffering are an inescapable part of this life

God's Word encourages us to be prepared for suffering because trials are inevitable. In a classic passage on this subject, the apostle Peter gently tells his followers, "Beloved, do not be surprised at the fiery ordeal among you, which comes upon you for your testing, as though some strange thing were happening to you; but to the degree that you share the sufferings of Christ, keep on rejoicing, so that also at the revelation of His glory you may rejoice with exultation" (1 Peter 4:12-13).

Yet how many of us are completely unprepared when affliction strikes? Like a soldier unprepared for battle, our initial response to suffering is often inappropriate or counterproductive. Perhaps we would be wise to include something like this in our morning prayers: "Lord, if You allow affliction or suffering to come into my life today, help me to be prepared biblically to see each person and event as a gift from Your good hand. Please help me to be ready."

D.A. Carson notes that suffering is inescapable even for the believer:

> Despite the best efforts of the proponents of the health and wealth gospel, the fact is that Christians get old and wrinkled. They contract cancer and heart disease, become deaf and blind, and eventually die. In many parts of the world Christians have to face the blight of famine, the scourge of war, the subtle coercion of corruption. This is not to say that God does not sometimes intervene on behalf of His people in remarkable ways. It is to say, rather, that we, too, live in a fallen world and cannot escape participation in its evil and suffering.[2]

Understand that there is not always a direct link between suffering and individual sin

Something about human nature automatically assumes that when a person suffers, it must be the direct result of some sin in that person's life. That was the assumption of Job's first three counselors. Eager to explain why Job was suffering, they relentlessly assumed that Job's losses were his fault. God's eventual response to their words ought to give all of us pause: "My wrath is kindled against you and against your two friends, because you have not spoken of Me what is right" (Job 42:7).

The same dynamic was alive and well when Jesus' own followers pointed to a man blind since birth and asked, "Rabbi, who sinned, this man or his parents" (John 9:2). There was no place in their theology for innocent suffering.

Compare their view to that of the apostle Peter, who told his readers; "Keep a good conscience so that in the thing in which you are slandered, those who revile your good behavior in Christ will be put to shame. For it is better, if God should will it so, that you suffer for doing what is right rather than for doing what is wrong" (1 Peter 3:16-17).

Of course we should not overstate our point. The Bible asserts in many places that sin has consequences (cf. Proverbs 28:13; Galatians 6:7; Hebrews 12:7-11). However, you may have examined your heart and life during a time of suffering and found yourself unable to see any obvious way that you had been displeasing to God. You may have prayed and asked God to help you in that process (Psalm 139:23), and you may have even enlisted the help of other spiritual friends. If no obvious sin is discovered, then it is counterproductive for you to practice morbid introspection that fails to acknowledge the possibility of innocent suffering.

Rejoice because God offers something better than raw fairness

When I was growing up, I would sometimes accuse my father of being unfair. My dad, who was an accountant, was incredibly astute at keeping a running balance sheet on what he had invested in me. He would announce that he would be happy to begin paying me for mowing the lawn (or whatever I was complaining about at the time) as long as I was ready to reimburse him for the meals, clothing, housing, and other expenses he had covered in caring for me. It was not long into those conversations that I recognized I did not really want or need raw fairness, a simple accounting of what I truly deserved. What I really needed was ongoing grace.

During a time of suffering, have you ever said that God is not fair? Do you recognize that, on one hand, you are right? If God were fair, we would die as soon as we were conceived. The Bible is clear on these two points: we are conceived in sin because the sin nature is passed down through human procreation (Psalm 51:5; Romans 5:12-21), and the wages of sin is death (Romans 6:23). Anytime we think that God is not fair, our response should be, "And I am glad He isn't *simply fair.* I want and need a God who is gracious, merciful, patient, and kind."

What God offers in place of raw fairness is benevolent sovereignty. He promises to use every circumstance for our spiritual good as He seeks to conform us to the image of Christ (Romans 8:28-29). If we truly love God and are committed to fulfilling the purpose for which we were redeemed, we will trust Him in times of suffering, even when we have no idea why God has allowed it to happen.

> What is God's purpose for me? Is it to pack my life with pleasant experiences? What is the "good" that God is doing in my life and the "abundant life" the Bible promises? Here again, too often we view the purposes and promises of the gospel in terms of our personal happiness. We forget that the gospel is more about the coming of Christ's kingdom than our individual enjoyment. God's main goal—the chief good He offers us—is to deliver us from the bondage of our evil desires and to make us participants in His divine nature. He is changing our heart—how we live and what fruit we bear. His focus is eternal and spiritual.[3]

Let suffering deepen your walk with God

Puritan pastor Richard Baxter taught that "suffering so unbolts the door of the heart, that the Word has easier entrance."[4] One of the ways to empty Bucket One is to allow each episode of suffering to draw you closer to the Lord. Consider these promises from Scripture to those who are afflicted:

> For the needy will not always be forgotten,
> Nor the hope of the afflicted perish forever.
> (Psalm 9:18)
>
> The afflicted will eat and be satisfied;
> Those who seek Him will praise the LORD.
> Let your heart live forever!
> (Psalm 22:26)
>
> This is my comfort in my affliction,
> That Your word has revived me.
> (Psalm 119:50)
>
> I know that the LORD will maintain the cause
> of the afflicted
> And justice for the poor.
> (Psalm 140:12)
>
> For the LORD takes pleasure in His people;
> He will beautify the afflicted ones with salvation.
> (Psalm 149:4)

Friend, have you allowed suffering, as Richard Baxter said, to unbolt the door of your heart so that the Word of God can have easier entrance? This might be a significant turning point as you learn to look beyond your pain to the truth of Scripture that can serve as a rich source of healing and help.

Face it hopefully

Perhaps one reason many of us would rather ignore or deny the pain of affliction is that we fear the outcome. We are unwilling to trust

God to use suffering to bring us to a better place in our relationship with Him. This is another way that both Asaph's and Paul's examples can be extremely beneficial. What they found is also available to us.

Your Redeemer stands ready to comfort you

Paul wanted the Corinthians to know that God "comforts us in all our affliction" (2 Corinthians 1:4). The word *comforts* in that verse means to "stand beside a person to encourage him when he is undergoing severe testing."[5] The God of heaven and earth stands ready to give us all the strength we need to handle suffering in a way that honors Him. In his book *Suffering and the Sovereignty of God,* John Piper says:

> God decreed from all eternity to display the greatness of the glory of his grace for the enjoyment of his creatures, and he revealed to us that this is the ultimate aim and explanation for why there is sin and why there is suffering, and why there is a great suffering Savior. Jesus Christ, the Son of God, came in the flesh to suffer and die and by that suffering and death to save undeserving sinners like you and me. This coming to suffer and die is the supreme manifestation of the greatness of the glory of the grace of God.[6]

I remember the days in the hospital as we were learning about our son Andrew's condition. At one point he had stopped breathing, and we feared for his life. In the quietness of the hospital room, I began asking myself, *Is there anything about this situation that God does not know? Is there anything about this situation that would render God unable to provide the grace and strength my wife and I so desperately need?*

As I prayed and contemplated these questions in light of Scripture, I found myself marvelously comforted. I was suffering because our little son's very life was in jeopardy. But during those days, God brought a peace to Kris and me that we would not trade for anything. Had we ignored or denied the pain, we would not have found the comfort that we so deeply treasure today.

He will not give you more than you can bear

Paul told the church in Corinth, "No temptation has overtaken you but such as is common to man; and God is faithful, who will not allow you to be tempted beyond what you are able, but with the temptation will provide the way of escape also, so that you will be able to endure it" (1 Corinthians 10:13).

The reason some of us do not embrace today's afflictions well is that we fear and worry about what tomorrow may bring. Living in such fear robs us of the very hope God offers when we choose to take Him at His Word.

Let suffering purify your heart

Hope in the midst of suffering comes in part because of the joy of identifying ways God wants to change us. Affliction offers us the opportunity to carefully evaluate our desires. Are our desires self-centered or God-centered? As Paul Tripp explains,

> Why do we question the faithfulness of God? Why do we think we are enduring more than we can bear? Why do we look for any escape we can find? Why are we not comforted by the promises of God? The answer is idolatry. Any situation that threatens my heart's desire for the things of this world will seem unbearable to me. God will seem unkind for placing me in that situation, and his presence will offer me little comfort.[7]

As you endure through a trial, what are your desires? Is God's glory your chief concern? Are you longing to be drawn closer to Christ? Do you eagerly seek ways to bless the person who is persecuting you (Matthew 5:44)?

Or are more sinister desires ruling your heart? Are you lusting after respect, ease, fairness, and immediate gratification? God would not want to remove the contents of Bucket One until we carefully examine the habitual desires of our hearts during times of suffering.

View suffering through the lens of eternity

We can also have hope because our suffering will last only a little while. I realize you might react strongly to that, especially if you are facing a trial that will probably continue for the rest of your life on this earth. I have many friends and church members in that same situation. Kris and I will likely have the lifelong privilege of caring for Andrew. But the key words here are "life on this earth." When we look at suffering through the lens of Scripture, we can experience great hope because even the longest trial on earth is brief compared to eternity.

> In this you greatly rejoice, even though now for a little while, if necessary, you have been distressed by various trials, so that the proof of your faith, being more precious than gold which is perishable, even though tested by fire, may be found to result in praise and glory and honor at the revelation of Jesus Christ; and though you have not seen Him, you love Him, and though you do not see Him now, but believe in Him, you greatly rejoice with joy inexpressible and full of glory, obtaining as the outcome of your faith the salvation of your souls (1 Peter 1:6-9).

Face it missionally

Both Asaph and Paul were able to endure suffering in part because they looked forward to the day when they could serve as a channel of God's comfort to others who were afflicted.

> But as for me, the nearness of God is my good;
> I have made the Lord God my refuge,
> That I may tell of all Your works.
>
> (Psalm 73:28)

> If we are afflicted, it is for your comfort and salvation; or if we are comforted, it is for your comfort, which is effective in the patient enduring of the same sufferings which we also suffer; and our hope for you is firmly grounded,

> knowing that as you are sharers of our sufferings, so also you are sharers of our comfort (2 Corinthians 1:6-7).

My experience as a pastor has taught me that often when God allows people to suffer, He is simultaneously preparing other people who will need their ministry of comfort in coming days. Men and women who have learned to practice authentic suffering in their own lives can in turn be used of God in unique ways to "bear one another's burdens, and thereby fulfill the law of Christ" (Galatians 6:2).

I encourage you to pause and ask God to help you suffer well so that when a fellow sufferer crosses your path, you can reach out to that person with the grace and strength you developed as you practiced authentic suffering in your time of need.

Organizing the Past

In what occurred, you were…

You responded…	INNOCENT	GUILTY
WELL	 BUCKET 1 The innocent past when you responded well requires: **Authentic Suffering** • ***Face it honestly.*** (Psalm 73:2—*But as for me, my feet came close to stumbling, my steps had almost slipped.)* • ***Face it biblically.*** (Psalm 73:17—*Until I came into the sanctuary of God)* • ***Face it hopefully.*** (2 Corinthians 1:3—*the Father of mercies and God of all comfort)* • ***Face it missionally.*** (2 Corinthians 1:4—*so that we will be able to comfort those who are in any affliction)*	
POORLY		

Emptying Bucket One

In this chapter we have begun to scratch the surface of what God teaches us in His Word about suffering. We do not have to face trials in our own wisdom and power alone.

That does not mean that the event that caused the suffering will magically disappear or even that the pain will ever be entirely erased. Rather, we have the promise that you and I can truly grow from the past. God can use times of suffering to draw us closer to Him and to prepare us to love others who are hurting. When we have taken the steps outlined in God's Word and benefitted from the trial as God desires, we can consider Bucket One to be empty.

For Jill

Jill had spoken to numerous counselors over the years and had taken many combinations of psychotropic medications. But her depression persisted and was getting worse. She feared that unless something changed, she would literally not survive the following winter.

Jill also had been trying to cultivate her spiritual life. However, she had not yet connected the dots between her depression, her past, and her relationship with the Lord.

It was time for Jill to reach into Bucket One. It was time for her to learn and practice the biblical principles of authentic suffering.

Jill's response to this encouragement was twofold. On one hand, she was quite reluctant to talk about her past. Because she had told those stories so many times before, she hoped there was a way to find healing without reviewing her past again. She was almost like the person holding shut the door to a closet overflowing with disorganized junk. Walking away and hoping things get better simply will not work. Someone has to open the door, sort the items, throw away what's useless, and carefully organize the rest. At the bottom of her heart, Jill knew this.

On the other hand, Jill was beginning to have hope. One day she said, "I know God can help me deal with this abuse properly." The principles and promises of God's Word were giving her confidence that this job really could be accomplished. She was also appreciative of our counselors, who were willing to help her lovingly and carefully as she sought to apply biblical truth to her life.

Jill was heartened by the truth that God had invited her to express her questions, fears, frustrations, and hurts. Somewhere along the way she had concluded that God was like some of the other men in her life—too busy or preoccupied to care about her. The notion of God as a heavenly Father who deeply and unconditionally loved her was a source of profound encouragement. She was slowly moving toward the position of the psalmist who, with a hope-filled heart, could say, "You have been my help, and in the shadow of Your wings I sing for joy" (Psalm 63:7). This was new ground for Jill—but it was good ground.

The more Jill cried out to God, the more interested she became in listening to Him. She began to process the pain of her past in a biblical way. The events themselves were not going to change, but the way she interpreted and viewed those events could. "I've never thought about suffering like that before" was something Jill frequently said as we studied Scripture together. It was almost as if she took off the glasses that caused her to view her life in a distorted manner and put on glasses that helped her to see the events in a more biblical light. Seeing her past from God's perspective was instructive and even liberating for her.

As this process developed week after week, Jill found what God promises in His Word—comfort. The more she used the lens of Scripture to see herself, her life, and even those who had mistreated her, the more she was able to find direction and peace. There was still more sorting to do. But she was now moving ahead with a growing relationship with her comforting Savior.

Questions for Personal Reflection

1. On a scale of 1-10, how would you rate yourself when it comes to suffering authentically? Are you growing in your ability to suffer well?

2. What do you see when you look into your Bucket One? Is it full? Empty? Somewhere in-between?
3. Earlier we studied the following ideas about suffering and hope:

    - Your Redeemer stands ready to comfort you.
    - He will not give you more than you can bear.
    - Let suffering purify your heart.
    - View suffering through the lens of eternity.

    What practical steps could you take to make these biblical truths more prominent in your heart and mind during times of suffering? What changes would occur in your life as a result?

Questions for Group Discussion

1. How do churches sometimes contribute to the fallacy that big boys don't cry? How serious a problem is this in light of the Scriptures we have studied in this chapter?
2. What does it mean to be a Christian friend to a fellow sufferer? What does that kind of person sound like, feel like, and act like? What are the benefits of being such a person? What are the risks?
3. Share with your group a situation in your life in which you processed your hurt or disappointment in a way that resulted in receiving comfort from Jesus Christ.

Illustrating the Principles

I love being a pastor. I tell people all the time that I am living my dream, and I sincerely mean that. One of the privileges of serving the Lord in this way is that I have the joy of watching Him not only "begin a good work" in men and women, but "perfect it until the day of Jesus Christ" (Philippians 1:6).

I realize that for some readers, the principles we are studying together in this book might seem difficult or even impossible to apply. That is why I have included four "case studies" to illustrate each of the four buckets. These are true stories of a person or couple who has grown from the painful experiences of their past (in some cases, names have been changed).

Please do not think of these vignettes as exhaustive discussions. Instead I hope to provide opportunities for you to think about how the four buckets are different from one another. Perhaps that will help you continue to process troubling events from your past.

Case in Point One

Receiving and Then Providing God's Comfort: A Picture of Authentic Suffering

Christine and Shane have been married for six years. God brought them together after Christine's first fiancé died unexpectedly just one week before their marriage. After Shane and Christine were married, God allowed Christine to become pregnant with quintuplets. After a difficult pregnancy, two of the infants died at birth.

Our pastoral staff had the privilege of walking through these events with Christine and Shane, and we marveled at the strength the Lord provided. While I am not suggesting they are perfect, in many ways their life experiences exemplify the principles of authentic suffering explained in chapter 6.

Another couple, Jamie and Jamie, are often affectionately referred to as Mr. Jamie and Mrs. Jamie among our church family. Mrs. Jamie struggled with cancer as a teenager and as a result was told she would be unable to have biological children. But after she and Mr. Jamie had been married for nine years, she became pregnant with twins through fertility treatments.

The doctors explained from the outset that this was a high-risk pregnancy because of Mrs. Jamie's past history of cancer. I'll never forget the day we received word that the first unborn infant had died. Mrs. Jamie was immediately taken to a specialty hospital where she was placed on complete bed rest. Even so, a few weeks later, their second infant died as well.

When I visited in the hospital shortly after their second baby had died, Mrs. Jamie told me that while she was thankful for the ministry of many of the people from our church family, they had been especially helped by Christine and Shane. Immediately I thought of 2 Corinthians 1. Because Christine and Shane had suffered well and eventually found comfort in Christ during times of tremendous loss, they were well positioned to become a significant source of comfort for Jamie and Jamie.

I asked these two couples if I could share their stories, and they graciously said yes. Our goal in doing this is not to magnify people but to glorify God, who gives strength, comfort, and hope to men and women who choose to suffer well.

Shane and Christine

Christine, tell us about your first fiancé and the events that led up to his death. What sustained you during those days?

Christine: Stan and I met in graduate school. I deeply admired his leadership abilities, his intellect, his humor, and his love for the Lord. During our final year of school we began dating. After graduating and working for a time, we were engaged and began planning our wedding.

One week before the wedding, while Stan was at my home, he said didn't feel well. He couldn't describe the symptoms, but he left for his apartment. About three to four hours later, in the middle of the night, I received a phone call from Stan. He said he couldn't breathe and couldn't get warm, and he asked if I would come over. Once I got to his apartment, I took him to the hospital. He was able to walk in by himself, but within 45 minutes he went home to be with the Lord. Autopsy results said he went into respiratory distress, but no one could determine why he stopped breathing. Thankfully the "how" of his death hasn't been something I've needed answered.

Here are some of the things that helped me get through the following weeks and months:

- Prayer, spending time with God
- Scripture reading, reviewing verses on cards
- Comfort of the Holy Spirit
- Journaling
- Reviewing sermon notes from a series about trials
- Godly friends: phone calls, prayers, spending time with me, sharing their wisdom
- Counsel from a pastor and his wife
- Serving others: hosting parties, hosting showers, letting others use my home
- Having fun and doing activities with the career class at church
- Receiving meals
- People helping with daily tasks such as mowing the lawn

Shane and Christine, how did God bring the two of you together, and how did Christine's past suffering affect the early days of your relationship? How were you able to build an effective marriage after Christine had suffered so greatly?

Shane: I arrived in Lafayette in 2001 and a friend invited me to start attending Faith Baptist Church. I got plugged into the career class, where I met Christine and Stan. I got to know them through class activities, and I became friends with both of them. It was only a few months later that Stan passed away.

I knew Christine would be hurting in ways I couldn't imagine, so I just tried to find little ways to encourage her, like fixing or moving things at her house, staying positive in conversations, and keeping her included in group activities. Over the following year we became better friends, and eventually agreed that dating was a good thing to do—dating with the purpose to get married. We were engaged just two months later and married four months after that, in October 2003.

There were things about all these events that helped our relationship grow stronger. We started off with a sense of respect and seriousness for God's purposes in dating and marriage that is not as common these days, so our commitment to each other and to God's way of doing things was strong. Having helped Christine deal with her loss made me grow more sensitive to her thoughts and feelings. I also found a great deal of respect for her ability to look to God in times of need and to rely on Him for hope, encouragement, and endurance. "An excellent wife, who can find? For her worth is far above jewels" (Proverbs 31:10).

Christine: We didn't let Stan's death create conflict in our relationship. I was able to talk about Stan's death and the memories I had with him, and Shane did not become jealous or angry. We were growing our friendship and building our own memories without dwelling constantly in the past. I was and am so thankful for Shane. I tried to use the reminder of the possibility of losing someone at any time as motivation to show kindness and respect to Shane.

What was it like to find out that you were expecting five babies?

Christine: We were thrilled to discover I was finally pregnant! However, I was fearful of the pain and possible complications of pregnancy, and I was scared that either none of them would make it or that they would all have severe disabilities. It was clearly explained to us that the odds were not in our favor for a good outcome.

Shane: I wasn't fearful, but I geared myself up for the challenges that were ahead of us. We had struggled to get pregnant, and we were considering adoption as the next step for our family. Instead, God provided sooner and much more than we had expected. The Lord had shown His faithfulness to us in the past, and I was confident that His faithfulness would continue with us in this trial. I believed that if God would set such a great challenge before us, He would also provide the means to use it for our good.

When did you first learn that the babies' lives were in danger, and how did you cope with the fear and uncertainty?

Christine: At an ultrasound appointment around 11 weeks, it was revealed that Baby A had lost his amniotic fluid. We were told that even though he might survive in the womb, he would probably not survive long after birth, and if so, would have severe disabilities. Although saddened, we trusted that the Lord would do what was best for Baby A.

At around 20 weeks I was hospitalized due to increasing contractions. I spent the rest of the pregnancy on bed rest in the hospital. During this time, I struggled with fear. Shane's consistent trust in the Lord and his gentle reminders of the Lord's faithfulness were a lifeline to me. The physical challenges became increasingly difficult, and we took things day by day. We listened to godly counsel from pastors, friends, and doctors. We enjoyed visits and meals brought by friends and family. We read Scripture, posted verse cards on the wall, prayed, and listened to some recorded sermons. Overall, we weren't sure how things would turn out, but we rested in the fact that God is faithful and focused on God's character and the possibility of a good outcome.

Shane: We continued counting the weeks. At 28 weeks Baby A's condition started to get worse. It was also much more difficult for the doctors to keep the contractions under control. We were advised to go ahead with a C-section delivery, and we decided to do so. Baby A, whom we named Matthew, lived for only a few hours before going home to the Lord. We thanked God for allowing us to have that precious time with our son.

How did you get through this terrible loss?

Christine: Another one of our boys, Isaac, did seemingly well through the pregnancy. However, because of his premature birth and possible complications in the womb, he was born a very sick little boy. Despite good medical treatment, his condition deteriorated and he died at three days old. Losing Isaac was more difficult than losing Matthew because we weren't prepared for it. I wondered if this was the beginning of all of them dying, and I couldn't imagine losing all five of my children at this point.

Shane: We were helped by good counsel from our pastors and deacons as we sought to make decisions that aligned with what God wanted us to do at each step. We focused on doing the best we could in the circumstances given to us so we could look back and know we tried to do what was right with the proper motives. If we hadn't done so, we would have set ourselves up for regrets and guilt that could later lead to bitterness.

Our other three children, Joshua, Abigail, and Elizabeth survived, and by God's grace are growing bigger every day.

Mr. Jamie and Mrs. Jamie

Mrs. Jamie, tell us about your struggle with cancer.

I was diagnosed with leukemia in August 1994 at the age of 16. Being a typical teenager, my first concern was that I might lose my hair, not to mention my life. I was in and out of the hospital for over a year, and during that time I had chemotherapy, radiation, and two bone marrow transplants. I finally went into remission in October 1995.

Throughout the entire time that I was suffering, I had peace. I knew that if I died I was going to heaven to be with the Lord. I had trusted Christ as my personal Savior three years earlier at a Christian summer camp. I remember the last day I was in the hospital. The doctor told me that I would never be able to have children because the radiation had done damage to my ovaries. Though I went through a lot of physical pain during my battle with cancer, the emotional pain of learning I would not be able to have children is what I remember most vividly. I knew even at the age of 16 that I eventually wanted to be a mom. Though I didn't know it at the time, God was preparing my heart, even as a teenager, to suffer well as an adult.

How did God bring you two together, and what impact did Mrs. Jamie's past bout with cancer have on your relationship?

Mr. Jamie: We met at the college/career class at church and were friends before we began a dating relationship. As we began dating I learned about the dramatic impact Jamie's suffering had on her relationship with God. This made me love her all the more because, though she bears many scars from the cancer, God's Spirit has produced a beautiful work in her because she suffered well. We were married on May 20, 2000.

What was it like to learn you were expecting twins but also that the doctors believed the pregnancy was high risk?

Mrs. Jamie: We were ecstatic when we found out we were pregnant. Two weeks later, we learned we were expecting twins. We were overjoyed! We had waited for a child for so long and just couldn't believe God had blessed us with two. We knew from the beginning the pregnancy would be high risk, but our trust and hope was in our Lord. We knew he had a perfect plan for us and our babies. We decided not to worry but to trust God for the results.

Shane and Christine

Even though Mrs. Jamie was expecting twins in a high-risk situation, you chose to minister to them. What motivated you to use the difficulties of your past in that way?

Christine: Simple—we love them! We have known them for nine years and have participated in the same class at church as well as some small groups. Through these encounters we have grown to love the Jamies. Many people loved and served us during our pregnancy, and we wanted to do the same for them. We wanted to make their hospital stay more comfortable and help them pass the long days on bed rest.

Shane: We remembered the grace God had shown us before. God sent people to us to encourage us as we waited, so how could we not encourage our friends as well? Some of the same gifts we received we passed along to them—things like spending time with them and their visiting family, bringing food and other practical items, and giving tips about dealing with treatments and hospital staff. We experienced the impact that even little things done in love can have, so we knew how much that would help the Jamies.

Mr. Jamie and Mrs. Jamie

What was it like to have a husband and wife who had experienced significant trials in the past minister to you in your time of need?

Our friendship with Shane and Christine has grown over the years. Looking back now, we can see how God perfectly positioned them to minister to us in our time of need. They were a great source of comfort and encouragement. We knew they understood what we were going through. They were 2 Corinthians 1 in action.

Mrs. Jamie, you and Christine spent a lot of time together while you were in the hospital. What did Christine say or do that especially ministered to you?

Christine's ministry to me began long before I was in the hospital. I marvel at God's perfect timing—He allowed our friendship to blossom during the year before my pregnancy. Christine was very helpful to me when I was in the hospital. She brought me Bible verses written out on cards and she encouraged me through visits and phone calls. Seeing how she had suffered well in her past gave me hope that I could glorify God through my suffering as well.

Mr. Jamie, you and Shane spent a lot of time together while Mrs. Jamie was in the hospital. What was it like to have a friend who had suffered in similar ways?

On the day that Jamie was losing the second twin, Shane and Christine came to the hospital with food for all of our family. It was such a blessing and comfort to me knowing they were there. The simple sacrifice they made to clear their schedule and make themselves available was better than anything I could ever have asked them to do. Their friendship during our trial really made an impact on us and on our family. Our family saw the love that Shane and Christine had for us, and I know God was glorified as our family witnessed their actions.

Shane and Christine

After the Jamies lost their babies, you two were right there with them. How did you find the strength to serve them in light of your past suffering?

At this point, it wasn't about us or the pain we had felt in the past; it was about meeting a need and loving people by sharing in their suffering. We could help them work through the grief of their loss or the fear of their unknown future by sharing what we had experienced. We could become an example of hope to both them and their extended family that this did not have to cause bitterness of heart, but could draw them closer to God and to each other.

Mr. Jamie and Mrs. Jamie

What counsel would you give to people who have unaddressed suffering?

Our message to anyone in this position is that there is hope for you. That hope is found in the perfect Word of God. Passages like Romans 15:4 and Psalm 119:49-50 assure us that our hope is found in God's Word.

John MacArthur in his commentary on Romans 15:4, says, "Without the clear and certain promises of the Word of God, the believer has no basis for hope." In order for us to claim these promises or even to understand them, we must have a right relationship to the One who gave them. One of the passages we turn to often is Romans 8:28, which assures us that God will cause all things, including any suffering from our past, to work together for our good. It also tells us who this promise applies to: "those who love God...those who are the called according to His purpose." Once we have a relationship with God through Christ we can be honest with Him about our suffering and experience healing at the deepest levels.

The only reason Shane and Christine were able to suffer well in their past and then comfort us in our time of suffering was because of their relationship with Christ and faith in His Word. Our hope is that anyone who has unaddressed suffering from their past will turn to the One who promises hope and will put their faith and trust in Him.

Shane and Christine

What counsel would you give to people who have unaddressed suffering?

God has a purpose for the trials and heartaches you have experienced. Part of that purpose is to mature you, and part of that purpose is to work good in the lives of others. We could have allowed the challenges of our high-risk pregnancy and the deaths of two of our boys to cause us hopelessness, anger, and bitterness that would have soured our marriage and other relationships. Had we done that, we would have had nothing to offer the Jamies in their time of need, and we would have had nothing in our hearts to offer back to our great and wonderful God.

Instead, with help from God's Word, we handled the suffering well and were able to share the help and hope God provided. We became evidence of His faithfulness and grace at work in the lives of His people, an example of His love for His children. God is ready to provide opportunities for you to handle your suffering well. Seek God in the Scriptures and through pastoral counsel, and He will show you what He wants you to do. He will help to heal your wounds, and He will open doors for you to share with others and minister to them.

Chapter Seven

Authentic Suffering and the Sustaining Gospel

My mother is a godly woman who has had a profound effect on my life spiritually. After my father died several years ago, Mom moved to the town where I pastor and has since become a delightful and joyful servant in our church. It has also been a tremendous blessing for my wife and our children to have "G-ma" (as my son Andrew affectionately calls her) live so near to us.

My mom had fifteen brothers and sisters. They grew up taking care of one another and maintained close contact as adults. But within the last eighteen months, four of my mother's siblings have died. We are entering the time of life with that generation where the sorrowful family events often outnumber the joyful ones.

The most recent death was that of my aunt Mary, who was five years younger than Mom. They loved each other dearly and spoke on the phone multiple times each week. They even shared an uncanny resemblance. It is hard to hear anyone cry, and it is even harder when it is your own mother.

My mom now faced a new challenge in her walk with Jesus. Her choices in response to this tragedy would become part of her past, for good or ill.

One of the Primary Goals of This Book

In the last chapter we learned that Bucket One is empty when you can say that you have processed your innocent suffering in a biblical manner. That is not to suggest that the pain will be entirely erased or that in coming days you won't think about or even mourn what occurred. But the bucket is empty in the sense that you have taken the steps outlined in the Word of God. You can truly say that you are handling your part of the problem.

The next question becomes, Are you prepared to process the next round of suffering, whether it is an unexpected reminder of what occurred or some new challenge or difficulty? In addition to helping you grow from your past, the goal of this book is also to equip you to face future trials in a way that keeps the bucket empty.

When I talk about being prepared to handle the next round of suffering, please don't think I'm advocating a cookie-cutter approach or simply giving you a list of instructions to follow in some rote manner. I agree wholeheartedly with Ed Welch when he writes, "Though many of us assume that change involves a plan with a series of steps, change on the heart level centers on knowing a person."[1] The goal of this chapter is to help us plan to respond to future suffering in a way that draws us closer to Jesus.

It's like the speech we gave our kids about cleaning their rooms. Most kids do not come out of the womb with an innate desire to pick up after themselves. You probably know what it's like to go into your child's room and not see the floor because of all the clothes, games, and candy wrappers lying around. After venting a few words of frustration for which you later had to ask forgiveness, you scheduled a time with your child to have a gigantic "clean up your room party." When the dust settled and the garbage company hauled away the dumpster, you looked at your child and said the words that practically every parent has uttered: "Now please *keep* your room clean."

That was sage advice. We have all learned as adults that it is easier to "clean as you go." The same truism applies to dealing with our past.

Emptying Bucket One is a good thing. Knowing how to keep it empty is even better.

It's also like losing weight. Unless you're one of those rare (and obnoxious) adults who can eat whatever you want and never gain a pound, you've probably had times when you went on a diet. And perhaps you were successful. If so, congratulations are in order. There is nothing easy about losing weight. But we all know the real struggle is keeping it off.

Losing weight is like emptying Bucket One by applying God's Word to whatever events have troubled you from the past. And keeping the weight off is like handling the next episode of suffering in a biblical fashion so the situation never even makes it to Bucket One. You process the trial properly before it becomes a destructive or debilitating part of your past.

One way people who have lost weight keep themselves motivated to not regain it is to remember the age-old adage, "Eat it today, wear it tomorrow." The temporary joy of eating that second slice of chocolate cake is not worth the long-term weight gain.

Why not use that same approach when we face times of suffering? "Do you really want to wear that?" is a legitimate question when we consider issues of the inner person, because:

- Today's reactions become tomorrow's habits.
- Today's choices become tomorrow's influences.
- Today's anger becomes tomorrow's bitterness.
- Today's thoughts become tomorrow's beliefs.
- Today's desires become tomorrow's idols.
- Today's decisions become tomorrow's consequences.

This was King Solomon's point when he said, "Watch over your heart with all diligence, for from it flow the springs of life" (Proverbs 4:23). As you consider your response to today's suffering, it is wise to get in the habit of asking, "Do I really want to wear that response, in my heart?"

The Power of the Sustaining Gospel

One key essential that will help you practice authentic suffering in coming days is learning to benefit from the *sustaining gospel.* This term is commonly used to describe that aspect of the good news of Jesus Christ that applies to the Christian life today.

Paul told the believers at Corinth, "I delivered to you as of first importance what I also received, that Christ died for our sins according to the Scriptures, and that He was buried, and that He was raised on the third day according to the Scriptures" (1 Corinthians 15:3-4).

Notice that Paul says the gospel was "of first importance." Earlier in 1 Corinthians he explained the centrality of the message of the cross when he said, "Christ did not send me to baptize, but to preach the gospel, not in cleverness of speech, so that the cross of Christ would not be made void" (1 Corinthians 1:17). C.J. Mahaney was right to observe,

> Paul simply refused to be pulled away from the gospel. The cross wasn't merely one of Paul's messages; it was the message. He taught other things as well, but whatever he taught was always derived from, and related to, the foundational reality that Jesus Christ died so that sinners would be reconciled to God.[2]

Some might say, "But I am already a Christian. Why should I still be concerned with the gospel?" Because the gospel has an impact on the way we live each and every day. In his excellent book, *A Gospel Primer for Christians,* Milton Vincent says,

> God did not give us His gospel just so we could embrace it and be converted. Actually, He offers it to us every day as a gift that keeps on giving to us everything we need for life and godliness. The wise believer learns this truth early and becomes proficient in extracting available benefits from the gospel each day. We extract these benefits by being absorbed in the gospel, speaking it to ourselves when necessary, and by daring to reckon it true in all we do.[3]

Exactly. As we learn to preach the gospel to ourselves every day, we are better prepared when times of suffering come. Some of the daily applications are radical because the gospel itself is radical. But if these principles are truly central to the message God has delivered to us in His Word, we can embrace them with the attendant promise that His Word is powerful enough to help us grow through even the toughest times of life. We can say with the psalmist,

> If Your law had not been my delight,
> Then I would have perished in my affliction.
> I will never forget Your precepts,
> For by them You have revived me.
> (Psalm 119:92-93)

That the topics of suffering and the sustaining gospel intersect is a significant emphasis in the Word of God. I encourage you to view the principles that follow as a beginning outline that you can develop in coming days.

Be Encouraged Because We Have a Crucified Savior

Charles Spurgeon said, "Abide hard by the cross and search the mystery of his wounds."[4] That is wise advice for men and women who wish to handle trials well. This aspect of the sustaining gospel gives depth, perspective, and meaning to our suffering.

His death proves His love for me

Paul explained to the Romans that "God demonstrates His own love toward us, in that while we were yet sinners, Christ died for us" (Romans 5:8). Later in that same book he proclaimed, "I am convinced that neither death, nor life, nor angels, nor principalities, nor things present, nor things to come, nor powers, nor height, nor depth, nor any other created thing, will be able to separate us from the love of God, which is in Christ Jesus our Lord" (8:38-39).

It is easy to feel unloved when someone is abusive toward you. But that is the time to look to the cross and remember your Savior's great love for you.

His death makes it possible to draw near to God

I often think about how difficult it must be for men and women to face hardships without a personal relationship with Jesus. It's this difficulty the writer of Hebrews had in mind after an extended discussion about the sufficiency of Christ's death, when he said,

> Therefore, brethren, since we have confidence to enter the holy place by the blood of Jesus, by a new and living way which He inaugurated for us through the veil, that is, His flesh, and since we have a great priest over the house of God, let us draw near with a sincere heart in full assurance of faith, having our hearts sprinkled clean from an evil conscience and our bodies washed with pure water (Hebrews 10:19-22).

When we suffer, it is wise to thank God for the provision He made in Christ so that we do not have to suffer alone. Because of the reconciliation made possible through the blood of Jesus, those who have trusted Christ as Savior and Lord are given the privilege of drawing near to God.

His death means that we do not have to sin as we suffer

As we grow in the Lord, it is important to learn the difference between "gospel indicatives" (*who we are* in Christ) and "gospel imperatives" (*what we do* for Christ). A classic example is the book of Ephesians, where the first three chapters extol our identity in Christ and the last three chapters explain our responsibilities to Christ. Trying to obey the Lord without understanding our position in Christ often leads to an external form of Christianity that is focused on busyness, activity, and duty alone.

One of the benefits of trials is that they make us realize we are in a position where there is very little we can do to help ourselves. We can't alter the bad diagnosis. We can't stop the harsh criticism. We can't dampen the pain.

But we *can* look to the cross. We *can* rejoice in our union with Christ's death. And we *can* recognize that because of this marvelous position, sin no longer has dominion over us and we do not have to respond in a sinful way. This was Paul's point in Romans 6:6 when he said, "knowing this, that our old self was crucified with Him, in order that our body of sin might be done away with, so that we would no longer be slaves to sin."

This aspect of the gospel is probably not foremost in our mind when we stand in line at a fast-food restaurant. But when we are suffering, the knowledge that we do not have to sin by complaining, lashing out, or becoming bitter is a liberating truth. Milton Vincent explains,

> The gospel is not simply the story of "Christ and Him crucified"; it is also the story of my own crucifixion. For the Bible tells me that I, too, was crucified on Christ's cross. My old self was slain there, and my love affair with the world was crucified there too. The cross is also the place where I crucify my flesh and all its sinful desires. Truly Christ's death and my death are so intertwined as to be inseparable. God is committed to my dying every day, and He calls me to that same commitment. He insists that every hour be my dying hour, and He wants my death on the cross to be as central to my own life story as is Christ's death to the gospel story.[5]

Learning to focus on the provisions of our crucified Savior during a time of suffering eventually becomes part of our theological DNA. By keeping Bucket One empty, we are well positioned to live life with the joy God intended even when life gets rough (Philippians 4:4).

Be Comforted Because We Have a Sympathetic Savior

Have you ever said to yourself during a time of trial, "No one understands the pain I'm experiencing"? Loneliness and suffering often go hand-in-hand. Yet in the midst of our loneliness we find opportunity to be comforted by the sustaining gospel. The Bible teaches us that because our Savior walked this earth and faced temptation, we now have a high priest who understands how we feel.

> We do not have a high priest who cannot sympathize with our weaknesses, but One who has been tempted in all things as we are, yet without sin. Therefore let us draw near with confidence to the throne of grace, so that we may receive mercy and find grace to help in time of need (Hebrews 4:14-16).

It is one thing for our friends and family members to extend sympathy during a time of suffering. Their willingness to do so is often a great source of help and strength. But that pales in comparison to the sympathy that the very Son of God offers us. Because He understands and sustains us, we can never truly say that no one understands. D.A. Carson observes, "The God on whom we rely knows what suffering is all about—not merely in the way that God knows everything, but by experience."[6]

One of the ways Jesus extends His sympathy as our Great High Priest is by praying for us. Spurgeon said,

> We little know what we owe to our Savior's prayers. When we reach the hilltops of heaven, and look back upon all the way whereby the Lord our God hath led us, how we shall praise Him who, before the eternal throne, undid the mischief which Satan was doing upon earth. How shall we thank Him because He never held His peace, but day and night pointed to the wounds on His hands, and carried our names on his breastplate.[7]

This is yet another truth we don't think about every day. But if we allow this aspect of the gospel to sustain us as we endure difficult times, we are better prepared in the days ahead to handle whatever trial may be next in God's sovereign plan for us. These kinds of choices become part of our past, and in turn our past becomes a helpful friend, not a depressing enemy.

Kris and I have experienced this repeatedly as we have faced the challenges of raising a special needs child. Not everyone understands what we have been through—how could they be expected to? But because our sympathetic Savior does understand, He provides all the help and hope we need.

Be Amazed Because We Have a Risen Savior

The greatest aspect of the gospel is that our Savior is alive. Scripture is clear that just as we were united with Christ in His death, we were also united with Him in His resurrection:

> We have been buried with Him through baptism into death, so that as Christ was raised from the dead through the glory of the Father, so we too might walk in newness of life. For if we have become united with Him in the likeness of His death, certainly we shall also be in the likeness of His resurrection (Romans 6:4-5).

Consider the phrase in the very center of that passage: "so we too may walk in the newness of life." Perhaps one of your biggest concerns about trying to apply the principles of this chapter is, "How can I know that the way I handle suffering can really be different?" Or, going back to the metaphors earlier in this chapter, "How can I keep the room clean and the weight off?" The answer is because of the power of your union with your resurrected Savior. That is why Paul told the Galatians, "I have been crucified with Christ; and it is no longer I who live, but Christ lives in me; and the life which I now live in the flesh I live by faith in the Son of God, who loved me and gave Himself up for me" (Galatians 2:20).

Did you know that when you choose to face hard times in this fashion, you are actually a living answer to a prayer request from the apostle Paul? In a beautiful explanation of the present-day implications of the sustaining gospel, Paul told the believers in Ephesus:

> For this reason I too, having heard of the faith in the Lord Jesus which exists among you and your love for all the saints, do not cease giving thanks for you, while making mention of you in my prayers; that the God of our Lord Jesus Christ, the Father of glory, may give to you a spirit of wisdom and of revelation in the knowledge of Him. I pray that the eyes of your heart may be enlightened, so that you will know what is the hope of His calling, what are the riches of the glory of His inheritance in the saints, and what is the surpassing greatness of His power toward us who believe. These are in accordance with the working of the strength of His might which He brought about in Christ, when He raised Him from the dead and seated Him at His right hand in the heavenly places, far above all rule and authority and power and dominion, and every name that is named, not only in this age but also in the one to come (Ephesians 1:15-21).

You can learn to call on your resurrected Savior to give you the power you need to face each day's difficulties with faith, grace, and love. Your union with Christ becomes stronger as you more consistently rely on Him.

Be Prepared Because We Have a Coming Savior

Because Jesus conquered death and ascended to heaven, we can expect him to keep His promise to return for His children (John 14:3). Christians are even promised a special crown for "all who have loved His appearing" (2 Timothy 4:8).

The sustaining gospel even allows us who are Christians to contrast the temporary length of our trials with the eternal glories of heaven. We agree with Peter when he said, "After you have suffered for a little while, the God of all grace, who called you to His eternal glory in Christ, will Himself perfect, confirm, strengthen and establish you" (1 Peter 5:10).

So ultimately it becomes a matter of comparison. Paul said, "I consider that the sufferings of this present time are not worthy to be compared with the glory that is to be revealed to us" (Romans 8:18).

Consider the way you typically respond when trials come your way. How much emphasis do you usually place on the truths of the sustaining gospel? Do you marvel at the cross and remember God's unfailing love for you? Do you peer into the empty tomb and rejoice in His great power? Do you look to the sky and think about how brief your suffering will be in comparison to the joys of the eternal home your resurrected Savior is preparing for you? Why not write some of the key verses mentioned in this chapter on index cards and carry them around with you. Seek to develop the habit of allowing the sustaining gospel to draw you closer to your heavenly Father as you suffer.

A living example

I mentioned in an earlier chapter how thankful I am for my wife, Kris, and the way she has parented our special needs son, Andrew, with such joy and grace. She is a testimony of the new life that God can powerfully put on display during times of suffering. You might wonder how Kris developed these abilities. To fully answer that question, we have to back up a generation.

Many people like to make mother-in-law jokes, but you will never hear one from me. Kris's mom, Irene, is a delightful Christian woman who has allowed God to demonstrate His power and grace through her during a time of significant suffering.

Over 30 years ago now, Kris's younger sister, Karen, was in a serious motorcycle accident that left her a quadriplegic. After months of hospital treatment, Kris's dad and mom chose to care for Karen at home. This may not be the appropriate choice in every similar case, but this is what Kris's parents chose to do. Kris's dad has since gone on to heaven, and Kris's mom continues to provide compassionate care for Karen.

What has always impressed me is the way Irene serves Karen with such abundant joy. She views her ministry to Karen as an opportunity to wholeheartedly serve Christ. She looks to her risen Savior daily for the strength she needs to minister to Karen well. Irene possesses a contentment and sense of grace that are rarely seen in the lives of people whose burdens appear to be far less.

This approach to trials has now become part of Irene's past. As a result she is free from bitterness, pity, and depression. Does that mean every day is easier for her? Certainly not. But Irene's crucified, risen, and coming Savior has proven Himself strong on her behalf day after day. Therefore she can say with Paul, "I am well content with weaknesses, with insults, with distresses, with persecutions, with difficulties, for Christ's sake; for when I am weak, then I am strong" (2 Corinthians 12:10).

Life breeds life

Kris and I thank God we have had the privilege of watching Irene serve Karen in this way. Her example has become a part of our past, enabling us to respond better to our trials. When the Lord then blessed us with Andrew, we were in a much better position to respond well. It is amazing how frequently Kris's treatment of Andrew mirrors Irene's treatment of Karen. In this way, the past has been a wonderful friend.

Just a little while

Both Karen and Andrew have trusted Jesus Christ as Savior and Lord. The day will come, and it may be soon, when Karen will be able to walk and talk and Andrew will be able to see. On that day, I believe Karen and Andrew will joyfully embrace their Savior who rescued them from their sin. And I also believe they will then go find their mommas. The hugs and joyful expressions of thanks from formerly special needs children for the faithful care of their mothers will be a delightful sight!

Yes, the sustaining gospel can help us handle suffering well. When we close the gap between our position and our practice, the result is simply beautiful.

Questions for Personal Reflection

1. Could you relate to the illustrations of how hard it is to keep a room clean or to keep the weight off? Why is long-term discipline such a challenge?
2. What steps can you take right now to prepare to handle well the next round of suffering? Write out a few of the typical trials you face and explain how the truths of the sustaining gospel could alter the way you often respond when hard times come your way.
3. In this chapter, what passages of Scripture especially affected you? Are there other Bible verses you could add as you begin to build your biblical approach to suffering?

Questions for Group Discussion

1. Compare your "child's messy room stories." How hard was it to get the room clean? How long did it stay clean? Which was harder and why?
2. Discuss what it takes to keep Bucket One empty. Do you agree that today's choices become tomorrow's habits? Why and how should this motivate us to try to handle today's suffering well?
3. Brainstorm various aspects of the sustaining gospel that can offer encouragement and help during challenging times. Describe hypothetical situations where a suffering Christian might practically apply the truths of the gospel in the midst of their pain.

Chapter Eight

Humble Analysis: Reaching into Bucket Two

In his book *The Abolition of Man,* C.S. Lewis coined several unusual phrases, including the possibility of human beings becoming "troused apes," "urban blockheads," or perhaps most famously, "men without chests."[1] His concern was an approach to life and science where people lacked the ability or the will to make sound moral judgments.

Writing in 1943, the underlying issue of Lewis's book was the practice of eugenics, the study of improving the qualities of the human species through genetic engineering. This discipline was developed by Charles Darwin's half cousin, Sir Francis Galton, and formed the backbone of Adolf Hitler's view of the world. C.S. Lewis viewed eugenics as the abolition of man's moral reasoning. "Men without chests" were people who exercised military might or scientific advancement without concern for truth and moral values.

Thankfully, Hitler's Nazism was exposed and defeated. The horrors of the Holocaust are grim reminders of what happens when human beings abdicate the pursuit of moral truth and virtue, which is a fundamental aspect of being made in the image of God.

Can Human Beings Know and Act Upon Truth?

The question of whether people can and should be expected to make sound moral judgments has a dramatic impact on the way we face the challenges of daily living. For example, Kris and I once attended a case conference with our son Andrew's teacher, several of his therapists, and the school psychologist. The psychologist said we should not expect Andrew to control his emotional outbursts. She explained that the ability to control one's emotions evolved later in human development and that a special-needs child like Andrew could not control himself. She believed we could actually harm Andrew if we tried to teach him to control his anger using biblical principles.

Kris asked the psychologist what we should do if Andrew were to lash out at others while we were walking through a crowded shopping mall. If Andrew could not control his temptation to lash out, how could we ever take him out in public? The psychologist said, "Call out to the people around him and tell them to stay away because he cannot control himself." In other words, treat him like a trousered ape.

This advice may have been appropriate for children who had little or no brain function, but to apply that reasoning to *all* special-needs children is absurd. Our son has diminished capacity (don't we all?), but there is a huge difference between diminished capacity and no capacity at all. We refuse to treat our son as if he's an animal. He clearly has the ability to make moral judgments.

Back to the Garden

This abolition of man began all the way back in the Garden of Eden. After God created us in His image, He commanded us to joyfully submit to His rule by subduing ourselves and the creation around us (Genesis 1:26-31). This love for truth and willingness to take responsibility for our choices is essential to understanding what it means to be truly human. When we fulfill this purpose, we honor our God, who created us for His glory (Isaiah 43:7).

While in the garden, Adam and Eve committed two sins. First, they disobeyed God's simple command not to eat of the forbidden tree. This aspect of their story is almost universally known.

However, their response after their rebellious act was equally hellish. When God lovingly confronted them about their choices, they refused to take responsibility and began to blame their sin on each other. Instead of subduing themselves and their environment by joyfully submitting to the King, they were subdued by their own rebellion and unwillingness to face the truth. In so doing, they abdicated their God-given role in the world. They were behaving like "men without chests."

A Crucial Transition

This brings us to a critical point in our discussion of the past. In earlier chapters, we acknowledged the horrible abuses men and women have faced that were in no way initiated by their own choices. God, by His grace, has given us principles that can help us handle the grinding affliction that sometimes attends our journey in this sin-cursed world. Ultimately these principles lead us to greater communion with Jesus, our sympathetic High Priest who stands ready to comfort and sustain us in our weakest moments.

However, "being sinned against" is not the only part of our stories. The hard reality is that many of us are stuck in the past, at least in part, because when someone mistreated us, we responded in a sinful way. We have sometimes been so focused on the hurt caused by others' misdeeds that we have never taken the time to address our unbiblical responses.

This is the essence of Bucket Two—the innocent past when we responded poorly. While I would never want to minimize the hurt caused by others and the importance of addressing it, the tale of our past also sometimes includes wrong responses on our part.

Because we were made in the image of God, we were created to face this aspect of the story as well. "He who conceals his transgressions will not prosper, but he who confesses and forsakes them will find compassion" (Proverbs 28:13).

It is not easy to acknowledge your failures, especially when someone else sinned against you. But doing so is an important step to God developing you into the new person He desires. It is the polar opposite of the abolition of man—think of it as reclaiming the position you were created for.

You can also take heart that you have the resources of heaven to help you face the truth. God the Father revealed Himself to Moses as One who was "abounding in lovingkindness and truth" (Exodus 34:6). Jesus comforted His disciples with the assurance that He is "the way, the truth, and the life" (John 14:6). The Holy Spirit was sent to guide us "into all the truth" (John 16:13). God's Word is truth (John 17:17), and Christ's church is the "pillar and support of the truth" (1 Timothy 3:15). In a culture that promotes the abolition of man through abandonment of moral truth, God's children can take that ground back in part by acknowledging the truth about their pasts. Doing so requires *humble analysis.*

Understanding the Buckets

In what occurred, you were...

You responded...	INNOCENT	GUILTY
WELL	BUCKET 1 The innocent past when you responded well requires: **Authentic Suffering**	
POORLY	BUCKET 2 The innocent past when you responded poorly requires: **Humble Analysis**	

Beware of Selective Memory

The challenge to this part of the process is developing the ability to admit honestly our past failures. Many of us are far more proficient at remembering and rehearsing the abuses of others while minimizing or forgetting the ways we sinned in response.

My dad and his favorite wrench

My father's favorite tool by far was his adjustable Crescent wrench. One day when I was about eight years old, he was working on our family car and needed his Crescent wrench, which he could not find. He proceeded to accuse me of misplacing it and gave me quite a lecture about irresponsibility. A few days later, Dad told me that he had found the wrench in a place where he had previously been working. He admitted that his angry accusations against me had been unfounded.

While my father's initial behavior was wrong, it was not the only part of the story. There is also the issue of what I chose to do after my dad's accusation. Was it acceptable for me to yell, pout, whine, and wrinkle up my face? And even to this day, why is it so much easier for me to remember his failures rather than my own?

But what if the other person's sins were worse than mine?

I fully realize that many readers struggle with situations far more serious than the one about my dad and the missing wrench. However, the importance of facing your side of the issue is still true. Jesus said it this way; "Why do you look at the speck that is in your brother's eye, but do not notice the log that is in your own eye?" (Matthew 7:3). The reason your side of the equation is the "log" is that you can never see clearly enough to help someone else deal with the sin in their life until you have first dealt with your own.

The Importance of Humble Analysis

Practicing humble analysis when someone has sinned against you is a critical element of growing from your past. You need to ask at least six questions about the way you responded to someone's sinful treatment toward you:

1. Did you return evil for evil?

2. Did you develop bitterness toward God?
3. Did you develop an unbiblical view of people?
4. Have you developed an unbiblical view of yourself?
5. Should you confront the person who sinned against you, and if so, have you done it?
6. If you confronted the person who sinned against you and he asked forgiveness, have you granted it?

Because these questions are so important, let's consider each of them carefully.

Did you return evil for evil?

Romans 12:17-21 is another example of how much emphasis the Bible places on our past. Paul assumes some people will treat us in an evil fashion. The real question is, How did we choose to respond? Consider Paul's words carefully, then think about the choices you have made when someone mistreated you.

> Never pay back evil for evil to anyone. Respect what is right in the sight of all men. If possible, so far as it depends on you, be at peace with all men. Never take your own revenge, beloved, but leave room for the wrath of God, for it is written, "Vengeance is Mine, I will repay" says the Lord. "But if your enemy is hungry, feed him, and if he is thirsty, give him a drink; for in so doing you will heap burning coals on his head." Do not be overcome by evil, but overcome evil with good (Romans 12:17-21).

Returning evil for evil is always wrong

Part of the beauty of God's Word is that it is often so abundantly plain. "Never pay back evil for evil to anyone." This disqualifies us from making any excuses, shifting any blame, and minimizing our responses. Returning evil for evil is...evil.

Seeking revenge displeases God

It often hurts when a person mistreats us. Our natural inclination is to function as the heavenly payroll clerk. "I don't get mad; I just get even" is frequently worn as a badge of honor, even by the people of God.

Scripture clearly condemns that kind of behavior. "Never take your own revenge." Never? Not even when what that person said or did really hurt? Not even when my emotions are raging? Not even when I was embarrassed? Not even when something of great value was stolen from me?

Never.

This does not mean the person who sinned against you is absolved from all consequences

Revenge is primarily an issue of the heart. Sometimes the person who sinned against you must still be made to face the consequences. For example, in cases of physical or sexual abuse, the abused person may have to report the abuse to the church, to the civil authorities, or both. It is possible to do so without sinfully seeking revenge. The key question to ask here is, What is motivating me to report this abuse—the desire to please God or the desire to exact my pound of flesh?

This does not mean we must always be at peace with everyone

Paul places a delightful balancing statement in the middle of this discussion lest we misunderstand or misapply what he has written. "If possible, so far as it depends on you, be at peace with all men" (v. 18). Even after we have fulfilled all our responsibilities in the matter, we may not be at peace with the other person. God calls upon us to handle only our part of the issue.

You must attempt to overcome evil by actions of good

The Greek word translated "overcome" in verse 21 is a military term meaning "be victorious." God wants evil to be defeated by actions of good. If your enemy is hungry, feed him. If he is thirsty, offer him a drink.

Most of us do not respond with kindness to evil treatment from others because such ideas are foreign to our natural way of thinking. Also, we live in a culture that often prizes the joy of revenge. No wonder so many individuals' pasts are littered with examples of returning evil for evil!

But this is hard!

This is another great opportunity to profit from the power of the sustaining gospel. Paul spent the first 11 chapters of the book of Romans explaining that because of the finished work of Christ on the cross, it was possible for us to be forgiven of our sin and brought into union with Christ's death, burial, and resurrection. The climax of Paul's presentation occurs at the beginning of chapter 12:

> I urge you, brethren, by the mercies of God, to present your bodies a living and holy sacrifice, acceptable to God, which is your spiritual service of worship. And do not be conformed to this world, but be transformed by the renewing of your mind, so that you may prove what the will of God is, that which is good and acceptable and perfect (Romans 12:1-2).

Because you are in Christ, you have the power to do what is difficult. You don't have to respond to the evil of others in the same way the world around you responds.

Did you develop bitterness toward God?

Bitterness is anger turned inward. Some men and women practically have bitterness written on their faces. And when they talk, their words confirm the existence of a bitter heart. How do such persons get to that place? Often it is because of an inappropriate response to a hurtful event in the past.

In an earlier chapter I mentioned the story of Naomi. Her response to trials is a focal point of the book of Ruth.

Naomi suffered greatly as a result of living in a sin-cursed world

The first five verses of Ruth 1 are chilling in their succinct retelling of

Naomi's misery. She, her husband, and their two sons left Bethlehem because of a severe famine. They traveled to the foreign land of Moab, and by the end of verse 5, Naomi's husband and their two sons are dead.

No one would say Naomi was responsible for her trials in any way, shape, or form. But Naomi had a choice about how she would respond. She was about to place a cluster of thoughts, desires, words, and actions into the bucket of what would eventually become her past.

Naomi chose the path of bitterness because of her wrong view of God

A.W. Tozer said that "what comes into our minds when we think about God is the most important thing about us."[2] When Naomi and Ruth arrived in Bethlehem, Naomi's words to the women of the city clearly revealed the condition of her heart: "Do not call me Naomi; call me Mara, for the Almighty has dealt very bitterly with me. I went out full, but the LORD has brought me back empty. Why do you call me Naomi, since the LORD has witnessed against me and the Almighty has afflicted me?" (Ruth 1:20-21).

Label that "a Bucket Two that is overflowing."

Did you develop an unbiblical view of people?

Jesus told His followers that the second great commandment is to love our neighbors as ourselves (Matthew 22:37-40). Some people have trouble loving anyone in the same class of persons as their former abuser.

For example, some women who have been abused by men conclude, "All men are like that." As a result they have great difficulty interacting with men on any level. Others have been harmed by a member of a particular ethnic or religious group and have now judged every person in that group by that one individual's behavior.

Judging everyone on the basis of one person's choices is very unloving. This unbiblical way of viewing people can become a harmful part of your past. Conversely, choosing to love (1 Corinthians 13:1-4) even if you have been abused is one of the central aspects of Christian character.

My grandparents moved to Gary, Indiana, in the 1950s. They had grown up in southwest Virginia but were forced to move "up north" to find work. My grandfather took a job at a steel mill at a time when the racial tensions in the area were extremely high. One night, while my grandfather was working the midnight shift, a man who was from a minority ethnic group broke into my grandparents' house. Even though my grandmother stood barely five feet tall, this man still chose to beat her on the back of her head with the butt of his gun before proceeding to rob their home.

I always admired my grandmother's response. Even after that event, she continued to befriend her neighbors regardless of their ethnicity. She was known for her cooking and gardening, and she kept on sharing what God had given her with those the Lord placed around her.

Some of the abuses of wicked people are staggeringly evil. But God can give His children the power to continue to view and treat others in a loving fashion even if they are part of the same people group.

Have you developed an unbiblical view of yourself?

Often the abusive treatment of others comes in the form of words. "Death and life are in the power of the tongue" (Proverbs 18:21). We cannot control what others say to us or about us. But we can choose whether we will make those ideas part of the way we continue to think about ourselves.

My heart weeps when I hear some of my counselees tell about the treatment they received as children. It is hard to imagine how painful it would be for a child to be raised on a steady diet of comments such as these: "You were a mistake," "You're stupid," "You will never amount to anything," and "I wish you had never been born."

We cannot dismiss the damaging impact such words can have on a person's view of self, but at some point, we all must evaluate such statements in light of what God says about us. This is what Paul meant when he said, "Through the grace given to me I say to everyone among you not to think more highly of himself than he ought to think; but to think so as to have sound judgment, as God has allotted to each a measure of faith" (Romans 12:3). God can help you put off unbiblical ways of thinking about yourself and replace them with thoughts that are true.

Should you confront the person who sinned against you, and if so, have you done it?

We need to broach this matter very carefully. Some people have unfinished business in their past because they should have confronted a person who sinned against them, and they have not done so.

The phrase "should have confronted" should be kept in the backdrop of this entire discussion. Children who were abused or overpowered by grown-ups could not have been expected to respond like adults at the time of the abuse. Employees cannot always immediately confront a superior without following an appropriate process outlined by their company. My primary concern at this point is for people who, according to Scripture, clearly should have confronted the person who sinned against them but chose not to.

Confrontation is an important biblical principle

Jesus taught His disciples, "If your brother sins, go and show him his fault in private; if he listens to you, you have won your brother" (Matthew 18:15). Many of God's people respond to sins against them by ignoring the offender, cutting him or her off, or gossiping behind the offender's back. Such sinful responses leave the event in Bucket Two long-term. They also make it difficult—if not impossible—to relate to the person in the future.

If you have any question about the appropriateness of confronting a person who sinned against you, seek godly counsel. Situations like this sometimes need to be evaluated case by case. Significant discussion is required to determine if personal confrontation is appropriate. People who have been sinned against often require extended preparation before they can properly confront a person who has been manipulative and hurtful. This is especially true if the abuser still retains a position of power and authority. Often another individual from the church, preferably someone in leadership, should accompany the abused person to ensure that additional harm and manipulation does not occur.

If you were sinned against, the fact that you are even considering what God wants you to do now is a wonderful step in the right direction. You can confidently claim Christ's promise that, "if anyone is willing to do His will, he will know of the teaching, whether it is of God" (John 7:17). I have seen relationships miraculously restored because an individual was finally willing to break the ice and take the biblical step of lovingly confronting the person who sinned against them.

If you confronted the person who sinned against you and he asked forgiveness, have you granted it?

Jesus frequently spoke about the power and importance of forgiving others. He said in Luke 17:3-4, "Be on your guard! If your brother sins, rebuke him; and if he repents, forgive him. And if he sins against you seven times a day, and returns to you seven times, saying, 'I repent,' forgive him." Some men and women have responded to the hurts of the past by refusing to forgive those who sinned against them, even when the offending party has clearly and in some cases repeatedly requested forgiveness. This is another sure way to remain stuck in one's past.

The seriousness of this issue is also illustrated in Mark 11:25: "Whenever you stand praying, forgive, if you have anything against anyone, so that your Father who is in heaven will also forgive you your transgressions." This passage makes it clear that God's willingness to forgive us today is dependent on our willingness to forgive others yesterday. How much stronger argument would we need for keeping Bucket Two empty?

But what about those we've confronted who refuse to request forgiveness? We should still seek to develop a forgiving spirit toward them. Christ showed a forgiving spirit on the cross when He said of His abusers, "Father, forgive them; for they do not know what they are doing" (Luke 23:34).

Organizing the Past

In what occurred, you were…

You responded…

	INNOCENT	GUILTY
WELL	BUCKET 1 The innocent past when you responded well requires: **Authentic Suffering** • ***Face it honestly.*** (Psalm 73:2—*But as for me, my feet came close to stumbling, my steps had almost slipped.)* • ***Face it biblically.*** (Psalm 73:17—*Until I came into the sanctuary of God)* • ***Face it hopefully.*** (2 Corinthians 1:3—*the Father of mercies and God of all comfort)* • ***Face it missionally.*** (2 Corinthians 1:4—*so that we will be able to comfort those who are in any affliction)*	
POORLY	BUCKET 2 The innocent past when you responded poorly requires: **Humble Analysis** • ***Did you return evil for evil?*** (Romans 12:17-21) • ***Did you develop bitterness toward God?*** *(like Naomi in the book of Ruth)* • ***Did you develop an unbiblical view of people?*** (Matthew 22:37-40—*the second great command)* • ***Did you develop an unbiblical view of yourself?*** (Romans 12:3) • ***Should you have confronted the abuser and if so, have you?*** (Matthew 18:15-18) • ***If you confronted the abuser and he requested forgiveness, have you granted it?*** (Ephesians 4:32)	

Taking the Next Step

This part of the study is challenging for sure. But friend, you were made in the image of God, and as a Christian you are being remade in the image of Christ. Instead of the abolition of man feared by C.S. Lewis, you can face any of your sinful responses to the evil treatment of others head-on. Remember Paul's words: "Put on the new self, which in the likeness of God has been created in righteousness and holiness of the truth" (Ephesians 4:24).

In the next chapter we will continue to study what is involved in emptying Bucket Two. Then we'll talk about how these truths helped Jill. For now, we already have enough information, summarized in the chart above, to begin the process of humble analysis. Carefully review the six questions we have discussed. If God is revealing aspects of your past that you still need to address, why not pause and ask Him to give you the strength and grace to face the truth as the human being He designed you to be?

Questions for Personal Reflection

1. List some of the events that fit into Bucket Two for you. Do you find it easier to focus on the sins of others or on your sinful responses?
2. Of the six questions we studied together, which one is most convicting to you? If an event from your past is in Bucket Two, which of the six questions points out the way you most likely failed?
3. How and in what ways has this chapter helped you see ways you can grow from your past?

Questions for Group Discussion

1. Ask several people to share their own versions of the "Steve and his dad's wrench" story. Why is it so much easier to remember and focus on the failures of others?
2. Discuss in practical terms what "returning good for evil" looks like. Try a role play in which one person behaves in an evil fashion and another group member responds in a way that is biblically "good."

CASE IN POINT TWO

Facing the Need to Confront: A Picture of Humble Analysis

FRANK IS A YOUNG MAN who worked in a Christian organization. Tragically, his supervisor regularly belittled employees, blew up at them, and engaged in dishonest actions. Frank and his coworkers were unwilling to speak to their supervisor about his behavior. The organization became a revolving door as employees became disenchanted. Frank knew he had a responsibility to speak to his boss, but he was unwilling to do so.

This is what makes Frank's story different from the earlier story of Christine and Shane. Both cases were examples of innocent suffering. But Christine and Shane handled their trials well and allowed their past to become their friend. In contrast, Frank had a responsibility he refused to accept. His unwillingness to speak to his boss allowed problems to fester. Therefore, Frank's past was rapidly becoming his enemy. Here's the rest of the story in his own words.

Describe what you experienced in your first few months as in employee in this Christian organization.

I thought working in a Christian setting would mean "a little bit of heaven on earth." Boy, was I naïve. I knew the work would be hard and the pay would be low. I was prepared for all of that. However, I was shocked at the way my boss treated me and the rest of the staff.

Angry tirades became a normal part of our workday. We were subjected to almost daily doses of critical speech. Our boss was also unstable emotionally so you never knew which boss was going to show up to work. Some days he was happy and even generous. But then the next day he would bite your head off in a meeting in front of the rest of the staff.

At the time, did you believe you had any responsibility to speak to your boss about what was occurring?

There was no question in my heart that I needed to speak to him. We were a Christian organization and our founding documents stated that we were all committed to relating to one another in a biblical fashion. The belief and expectation was that we were to function as brothers and sisters in Christ regardless of our job classification. I agreed to these principles when I accepted my position.

I knew that Scripture outlined the steps I needed to take in response to my supervisor. For example, I often thought of Galatians 6:1, which says, "Brethren, even if anyone is caught in any trespass, you who are spiritual, restore such a one in a spirit of gentleness; each one looking to yourself, so that you too will not be tempted." I also knew Matthew 18:15: "If your brother sins, go and show him his fault in private; if he listens to you, you have won your brother." I realize there are different problem-solving processes in place at other organizations, but in my case I was clearly responsible to obey these verses and speak privately to my boss about my concerns.

Did you follow God's Word in this matter right away? Why or why not? How did your choices affect you and the overall situation at work?

I'm ashamed to say that I waited many months before speaking to my boss. Looking back now, I believe the central issue for me was fear. Proverbs 29:25, "the fear of man brings a snare," became a controlling verse for me. I was trapped in a situation that was increasingly hopeless because I was afraid to do what I knew God's Word commanded.

It also became a matter of obedience to Christ. On the one hand, I had the Lord's clear commands. On the other hand, I had all kinds of ideas and excuses that seemed reasonable to me. I had to decide if I was going to live according to God's Word or by my opinions. Over time, I became increasingly convicted about my disobedience to Scripture.

During these days and months, the situation at work continued to deteriorate. Whenever I saw another coworker berated, I wondered if that event could have been prevented if I had fulfilled my responsibility. It also seemed as though the Lord was not blessing our ministry, and I wondered if these unaddressed problems were grieving the Holy Spirit of God (Ephesians 4:30).

I became increasingly dissatisfied. I considered running away from the problems or quitting the ministry altogether. My past was quickly becoming my enemy.

Did you eventually decide to speak to your boss? What changed your mind? Describe what happened.

After several months I decided I had to take the steps outlined in God's Word and speak to my boss about these matters. Two ideas especially motivated me to act. First, I was convicted about my lack of obedience to God's Word. I had trouble reconciling how I said that Jesus was my Lord with my unwillingness to live life His way. I knew my boss's sin was wrong—now I had to face the fact that my inactivity was sinful as well.

I also concluded that my refusal to address this problem was unloving to my boss. He was a gifted man in many ways, but his sinful communication habits were hindering his ministry. The verse about how "perfect love casts out all fear" (1 John 4:18) motivated me to take the focus off myself and what I might lose and place it on serving God and my boss. I came to the conclusion that I could love both of them by seeking to address this problem in a godly, biblical, and loving fashion.

I eventually scheduled a time with my boss to discuss these matters. I prayerfully wrote out in advance what I would say. I had already asked God's forgiveness for failing to discuss this sooner, and I asked my boss's forgiveness as well. I then attempted to outline the ways I believed my boss had been sinful in his communication with me and others.

I was shocked at how my boss responded. He was clearly uncomfortable—I am fairly certain few people had ever been willing to speak so directly to him before. But the Holy Spirit was at work, and the biblical principles I mentioned had a profound effect on my boss. He thanked me for having the courage to speak to him and asked me to forgive him for his sinful speech. He eventually did the same with the rest of our staff and publicly committed himself to working harder on this in the future. I realized both then and now that the outcome could have been far different. But I was committed to finally doing the right thing and trusting God for the results.

Has it been hard to forgive your boss? What is your advice to anyone in a similar situation?

There are still times when I think about some of the hurtful words my boss said to me. And while there is evidence that he is seeking to do better, I recognize that no one changes overnight. But I believe that forgiveness involves a mental choice to "not remember" his former sins. The Lord does not want me to relate to my boss each day through the lens of his past failures. If God loves me enough to cast my sin as far as the east is from the west (Psalm 103:12), I can certainly show the same kind of love to the people around me.

The main lesson I learned here is to obey God's Word quickly. I let far too much time pass between my boss's sin and my willingness to respond biblically. I realize that there may be different processes in place in some employment settings, but in my case, the path was abundantly clear. I should never have allowed my failure to confront problems quickly become part of my past, and in the future, I am determined to communicate quickly and biblically.

Chapter Nine

The Joy of Forgiveness

This week I am scheduled to go to the dentist. He is a fine enough man—in fact, he's a member of our church. But I really do not want to go see him. Honestly, there are few places I would like to go less. Have you ever noticed that there were no dental chairs in Genesis 1–2 prior to the fall? Nor are they present in the Bible's description of heaven. Drawing on all my biblical and theological training, I conclude that dentists and dental chairs are a result of the curse.

We all know the experience. The hygienist lays you back in a chair and says, "Make yourself right at home." The real purpose of the chair is to get your feet as far from the floor as possible, making it harder for you to escape. Then she smiles brightly and asks you happy questions about your day. But the movements of her hands betray her expression as she deftly reaches for that tray of instruments. You know the ones I'm talking about—the sharp ones. Instruments of torture and terror.

Then the dentist arrives and begins performing unspeakable acts with those instruments—poking, prodding, causing pain and drawing blood. With a sinister grin he reaches for his drill and begins doing things to your mouth that long ago should have been outlawed in every civilized country on the planet.

In case I'm not making myself clear, I really do not want to visit the dentist this week. But I'll go, just as I do every six months or so. Why? There are at least two reasons.

The first has to do with those pictures on the wall. Have you noticed how sometimes the hygienist and dentist leave you alone in the chair with nothing to do but to stare at those pictures of tooth decay? "I'll brush more, I'll floss daily, I'll eat less sugar," you find yourself saying. But the dentist is right—you either deal with the small problems today or they will become bigger ones tomorrow.

The second reason is that experience you have as you leave the office. You run your tongue over your shiny teeth and enjoy the result of feeling really clean. Yes, it was hard. It even hurt a bit. But you're glad you went. It was the right thing to do.

The Last Chapter May Have Hurt a Bit

I realize that reading the last chapter may have felt like going to the dentist for you. Growing from your past is not all about focusing on the sinful treatment of others. Because you were made in the image of God, you can also face the times when your response to being sinned against did not please the Lord. That too is part of your story, and if those instances and habits are not addressed, they will result in *soul decay.*

The Bible doesn't have any color photos to depict this condition, but it certainly has some graphic language, such as these words from the pen of King David:

> O LORD, rebuke me not in Your wrath,
> And chasten me not in Your burning anger.
> For Your arrows have sunk deep into me,
> And Your hand has pressed down on me.
> There is no soundness in my flesh because of Your
>   indignation;
> There is no health in my bones because of my sin.
> For my iniquities are gone over my head;
> As a heavy burden they weigh too much for me.
> My wounds grow foul and fester

Because of my folly.
I am bent over and greatly bowed down;
I go mourning all day long.
For my loins are filled with burning,
And there is no soundness in my flesh.
I am benumbed and badly crushed;
I groan because of the agitation of my heart.
(Psalm 38:1-8)

These words make tooth decay seem mild by comparison. The good news is you do not have to remain forever with unaddressed sin festering in your soul and robbing you of the health and vitality God offers. And here's the greatest news of all: while this process is sometimes difficult, Jesus took the pain, the shame, and the guilt when He died in our place. What is left for us is to experience the joy of forgiveness. That is why David could also write:

Behold, You desire truth in the innermost being,
And in the hidden part You will make me know
wisdom.
Purify me with hyssop, and I shall be clean;
Wash me, and I shall be whiter than snow.
Make me to hear joy and gladness,
Let the bones which You have broken rejoice.
Hide Your face from my sins
And blot out all my iniquities.
Create in me a clean heart, O God,
And renew a steadfast spirit within me.
Do not cast me away from Your presence
And do not take Your Holy Spirit from me.
Restore to me the joy of Your salvation
And sustain me with a willing spirit.
Then I will teach transgressors Your ways,
And sinners will be converted to You.
(Psalm 51:6-13)

The goal of this chapter is to help make the process of emptying Bucket Two more attainable. When you deal with your sinful responses to others who hurt you, you will experience God's forgiveness and have the joy of your salvation restored.

The Challenge of Confronting Yourself

God has given me the privilege, as part of my pastoral ministry, to serve our church and community as a biblical counselor. I don't keep careful track of such matters, but I suppose I have spent over 10,000 hours counseling men and women in need. Those opportunities and relationships have enriched my life in many ways. Some of my former counselees are close friends today. But I have observed one universal trend in counseling: People rarely admit their sin to God and others.

I often ask counselees to describe the last time they asked God or another person to forgive them in some specific way. I am amazed at how frequently the response is dead silence—as if I had posed some sort of trick question.

This may explain why some men and women are so troubled by their pasts. The truth is that unaddressed sins against God and man are weighing them down like balls and chains. Yes, in some cases the problem may have been initiated by another person's sin. But until we handle our wrong response, the contents of Bucket Two will continue to plague us.

Several underlying spiritual issues often prevent us from confessing our sin to God and others. This part of the process is something akin to a spiritual root canal. But if that is what it takes to enjoy God's forgiveness more fully, most of us would close our eyes and say, "OK, let's start to drill."

Here are five reasons we struggle to admit our sin in the past:

- pride
- stubbornness
- fear
- foolishness
- misplaced desires

Not a pretty list, is it. But if any of these tendencies have influenced the ways we have sometimes handled our failures in the past, it would be best to face them honestly before our God. He stands ready to forgive us when we come to Him in repentance and faith. Let's think more carefully about the reasons we struggle to admit our past sins.

Pride

"Pride goes before destruction, and a haughty spirit before stumbling" (Proverbs 16:18). When someone else has provoked me in an evil way and I responded sinfully, I do not like admitting my fault. As I said earlier, there are few places I like less than visiting the dentist. One of them is visiting the place of contrition and confession. Most of us would rather do practically anything before admitting our sin. But the joy of forgiveness will never be experienced by the person whose heart is filled with pride.

Not long ago I conducted a staff meeting attended by 40 or 50 people. During the discussion someone said something I did not like. I responded with harsh and cutting words. This staff member loved God and me enough to speak to me about it later. He was right—my response did not please God. But why was it so hard for me to acknowledge my sin? The plain answer is this: Pride resides in my heart. I later asked this man's forgiveness, and because my response occurred in front of a group of people, I asked for their forgiveness as well. But I am still amazed at how hard it was for me to make such a simple acknowledgment.

Stubbornness

"Therefore if you are presenting your offering at the altar, and there remember that your brother has something against you, leave your offering there before the altar and go; first be reconciled to your brother, and then come and present your offering. Make friends quickly with your opponent" (Matthew 5:23-25).

Jesus' words could not be clearer. If you have sinned against another person in any way, stop whatever you are doing and make it right. "But they sinned against me first, or most, or whatever..." is no excuse for refusing to follow this biblical command.

I have counseled many people whose pasts were littered with broken relationships. If the counselee had responded sinfully to the failures of others, my counsel was simple: Pick up the phone or write a letter. Saying, "I sinned against you; would you please forgive me?" is often the first step to restoration with others. Stubbornly refusing to obey God's directives will make a bad situation worse.

Fear

Adam made an amazing statement in the garden when God confronted him about his sin. "I heard the sound of You in the garden, and I was afraid because I was naked; so I hid myself" (Genesis 3:10). Afraid? Of God? Where in the world did that come from?

I am convinced that many men and women allow fear to hinder them from acknowledging their past sin. Perhaps they believe the other person will use their confession against them. In some cases that may occur. However, you cannot know that in advance, and even if you could, you cannot allow fear to stop you from doing what God commands. Remember Paul's words to Timothy: "God has not given us a spirit of timidity, but of power and love and discipline" (2 Timothy 1:7). Fear can and must be overcome by a choice to obey God's Word and a belief that the joy of forgiveness outweighs the pain of confession.

Foolishness

"The way of a fool is right in his own eyes, but a wise man is he who listens to counsel" (Proverbs 12:15). We can easily manufacture dozens of reasons why our sin in the past was justified. "I don't need to confess that to God." "I don't need to speak to the person I sinned against." "His failure was so bad that my sinful response was acceptable." Reread Proverbs 12:15. Such ideas melt away in light of God's Word.

It's good to establish a spiritual friendship with someone who can help you evaluate your past sinful responses. "He who walks with wise men will be wise" (Proverbs 13:20). Asking a godly counselor to review your words and actions is sometimes hard, but it is a sure path toward wisdom and away from foolishness.

Misplaced desires

A refusal to admit our past sins often reveals desires in our heart that have taken the place of wanting to honor God. Here are some desires or idols of the heart:

- I must never make myself vulnerable by admitting my failures.
- I must have the approval of people.
- I must always have power over others.
- I must always have the upper hand.
- I must get back at the other person for what he did.
- I must never let that person hurt me again.

Sound familiar? Each of these desires—and so many more—will prevent us from taking steps to cleanse our pasts of any sin we committed in response to the mistreatment of others.

The Possibility of Being Forgiven by Others

Facing our side of the issue is always a challenge, especially when someone else initiated the problem. However, we should focus on how admitting our sins to other people can open up the possibility of forgiveness and reconciliation. "Behold, how good and how pleasant it is for brothers to dwell together in unity!" (Psalm 133:1).

Some might wonder what this process of emptying Bucket Two looks like. Here are a few hypothetical examples of how a person might approach someone they sinned against after the other person failed first:

- "John, I'm sure you remember the argument we had two weeks ago. Some of what you said hurt me deeply. But instead of coming to you and trying to solve the problem, I have stubbornly been giving you the cold shoulder. I've even looked for occasions to hurt you back with my words and actions. I realize now that God's Word calls such behavior 'returning evil for evil.' Please forgive me for treating you in this way. Can we talk now about what you said? I promise I'll try to listen carefully to your point of view, and I hope you'll do the same for me."

- "Mary, I know I've spoken to you in a very harsh way on several recent occasions. You asked me to forgive you for your failure several months ago, and I promised that I would. But instead, I've been brooding over what you did. I have even been gossiping behind your back. My proud refusal to forgive you has made it easy for me to justify my harsh words. Please forgive me for my sinful speech and also my refusal to forgive you when you asked. What you did hurt me, but that doesn't justify what I've been doing in response."
- "Sue, would you please forgive me for my bitterness? It was my responsibility as your father to model for you what it means to trust God even when it's hard. But ever since your mom died, I have lashed out at you and everyone else in my life. I'm ashamed to admit it, but because I was hurting, I wanted everyone else around me to hurt as well. I have even said several times in your presence that there was nothing left to live for. I realize now how hurtful those words must have been to you as my daughter, a precious gift from God to me. I know there are still some rough days ahead, but I promise I will work on replacing bitterness with passionate trust for our God. I want to be a better dad in the days ahead—would you please pray for me during this time of struggle?"
- "Frank, I know the way I've been putting you off sexually the last few months has been displeasing to God. I should've been more thoughtful to your needs as my husband. But ever since that man at work sent me that lewd email, I have really been struggling with the thought that all men are like him. Yet I have no reason to believe that about you, and it was foolish of me to be so cold to you. Would you please forgive me? Would you come with me to discuss this matter with my boss so we can properly address this problem with my coworker?"
- "Beth, you said in your Christmas card that you were sad

> that you hadn't heard from me for two years. You don't even realize this, but I haven't spoken to you because of a comment you made at our son's wedding the previous summer. But before we talk about your comment, would you please forgive me for not coming and talking to you about it sooner? I realize now that I was afraid of how you might respond. Maybe I just misunderstood what you said or perhaps your words were sinful. Either way, that doesn't justify the way I cut you off without even attempting to be reconciled. Would you please forgive me for letting sinful fear prevent me from doing what God wanted me to do?"

Those are just a sample of the kind of conversations that might result from a person genuinely seeking to empty Bucket Two. The possibilities are practically endless, but the common thread is the desire to handle your side of the issue.

One objection I've heard is, "But I know the other person won't forgive me, so why should I bother talking to him or her?"

The answer is twofold. First, we do not know for certain what the other person will or will not do. The Bible is filled with stories of unlikely people doing unpredictable things. Nothing is impossible with God (Luke 1:37). Second, we are responsible to do what God wants us to do regardless of the choices other people might make in return. We cannot force others to forgive us, but we can be sure we have done everything in our power to put them in the best possible position to do so.

Jesus said; "Be on your guard! If your brother sins, rebuke him; and if he repents, forgive him. And if he sins against you seven times a day, and returns to you seven times, saying, 'I repent,' forgive him" (Luke 17:3-4). This process works regardless of which side of the equation you are on because it was designed by Jesus Himself.

I cannot tell you how many times I have watched the words, "Please forgive me," melt the ice between two people. Often this simple act of humble obedience leads to the beginning of a restored relationship. It's like the feeling you have when you rub your tongue over your teeth as you leave the dentist's office. It wasn't easy, but the results are magnificent.

The Assurance of Being Forgiven by God

There is no guarantee that other people will quickly and joyfully forgive us when we admit our sins and ask their forgiveness. Obedience to God's Word sometimes makes us vulnerable and puts us at risk. That is part of what it means to take up our cross and follow Christ (Luke 9:23).

A new level of fellowship with Him

What we can count on is the way God will respond when we practice *humble analysis.* We can embrace the ironclad promise that we will enjoy forgiveness, cleansing, and enhanced fellowship with Him. Look at what the book of 1 John says about the delightful possibility of us enjoying increased fellowship with God:

> What we have seen and heard we proclaim to you also, so that you too may have fellowship with us; and indeed our fellowship is with the Father, and with His Son Jesus Christ. These things we write, so that our joy may be made complete (1 John 1:3-4).

It is amazing to think that ordinary men and women can truly have fellowship with the God of heaven and earth. And as we develop a warm, intimate relationship with our heavenly Father, our joy becomes complete.

The power of walking in the light

This kind of intimacy with God requires an approach to life that John goes on to describe as "walking in the light" (v. 7). This means dealing honestly and directly with our failures. That is why the passage also explains that if we say we have not sinned, we are lying and the truth is not in us. This principle is so important that it is repeated twice (vv. 8 and 10).

The foundation of walking in the light is found in verse 9: "If we confess our sins, He is faithful and righteous to forgive us our sins and to cleanse us from all unrighteousness." Confessing sin to God is not easy, but it is a key to enjoying fellowship with Him.

This is one of the reasons I wrote this book. I speak with many men and women who tell me they don't feel as close to the Lord as they would like. As they continue to unpack their stories, they often tell of times when other people hurt them. But they seldom share how they responded. That part of the story is often omitted.

I have found that passages such as 1 John 1 can help these people to think about ways they may have sinned in the process. Frequently they conclude that Bucket Two is rather full. No wonder they do not feel as close to the Lord as they desire. Fellowship with God comes from walking in the light. And walking in the light requires an open attitude toward admitting past sins. Those who confess their sin to God and others regularly have an empty bucket and try to keep it empty.

This brings us face-to-face with our Savior

John concludes his thoughts about fellowship with God and walking in the light in the opening verses of chapter 2:

> My little children, I am writing these things to you so that you may not sin. And if anyone sins, we have an advocate with the Father, Jesus Christ the righteous; and He Himself is the propitiation for our sins; and not for ours only, but also for those of the whole world (1 John 2:1-2).

This passage points out two crucial truths about our Lord and Savior Jesus Christ: He is both our *advocate* and our *propitiation.* As our *advocate,* He defends us when the enemy of our souls accuses us before the throne of God day and night (Revelation 12:10). And the basis of His defense is not our righteousness but His. He is our *propitiation* or satisfaction. When our adversary accuses us, and often rightly so, our heavenly lawyer points to the wounds in His hands and side. Then the holy Father raps the gavel and declares that our sin has been forgiven and the case is dismissed.

Confessing our sin is hard; it's like going to the dentist. But because of the person and work of Jesus Christ, our advocate and propitiation, we should regularly acknowledge our failures to God and others, and then quickly and joyfully embrace God's forgiveness and cleansing.

For Jill

Without a doubt, understanding the importance of *humble analysis* was a key turning point for Jill. She knew her parents were not right when they suggested that the problems of her past were all her responsibility. However, she had not found much help from her therapists, who had suggested for years that her struggles were everyone else's fault.

Jill's past was becoming more and more like a messy basement no one wants to tackle. But by this point in the counseling process, she had gained a fairly solid handle on the corner of the basement labeled "innocent suffering." She had learned much from Scripture about suffering, and she had begun to find genuine comfort from her sympathetic Savior.

Now it was time to move to another corner of the basement. I was amazed that Jill was almost excited to take the next step. Looking at a properly organized portion of the basement had given her hope that perhaps the rest of the mess could be sorted as well.

I remember the day we began discussing ways Jill might have displeased God in her response to the evil treatment of others. She looked at me and said, "You aren't going to treat me like a helpless victim, are you?" In other words, she wanted to face the truth about all aspects of her story. Of course we would do it slowly, gently, and compassionately. But Jill was right. She was not a helpless victim who was destined to remain depressed the rest of her days.

For Jill, this part of the story felt very much like going to the dentist. But in Christ, Jill could face the truth, and she did. She began to list the ways she had sinned in response to the sins of others. She did not take responsibility for their actions, but neither did she pass off responsibility for hers. For the first time in her life, she looked at her past through the lens of truth. And she found power in Jesus' promise, "You will know the truth, and the truth will make you free" (John 8:32).

Jill eventually concluded there were numerous ways she had displeased God in her responses to the abuse and disappointment of others. She made a list of these specific failures and confessed them to God. Eventually we set up a time during which she could both confront her parents for the ways they had sinned against her and confess the ways she had sinned against them. This was new territory for everyone involved, and the results were mixed. But Jill was delighted she had handled her side of the equation in a way that pleased the Lord. The tide was turning because Jill was determined to handle each aspect of her past God's way. Bucket Two was well on its way to being emptied.

Questions for Personal Reflection

1. How well do you confront yourself? When is the last time you can remember thinking about a situation from the perspective of how you may have failed?
2. How do you feel about confronting others? Is this an area of the Christian life you find easy to obey or hard? Why?
3. Are you a forgiving person? Explain your answer.

Questions for Group Discussion

1. Decide as a group which is easier: Going to the dentist or emptying Bucket Two? Why?
2. Role-play a situation in which a person has to confront another brother or sister in Christ.
3. Discuss the process of growing from your past. Are the members of your group finding hope as you systematically work through areas of your past with the help of biblical principles?

Section Three

Handling the Guilty Past

Chapter Ten

Joyful Remembrance: Reaching into Bucket Three

When I was learning to drive, my dad owned a car that had a manual transmission. Back in the olden days, we called that having "four on the floor," and it was pretty cool. For some reason, dad decided this was the car he should use to teach me how to drive.

If you've learned how to drive a stick shift, you know how challenging it can be at first. That's how it was for me. There were too many steps to concentrate on at once—push in the clutch, press down the accelerator, let off the brake, move the gearshift, and occasionally look up at the oncoming traffic. If you didn't synchronize all your steps just right, the car jolted forward and usually stalled. I practically wore out the clutch in my dad's car. I still marvel at his patience. He must have said a thousand times, "Let's try that again, a little slower this time."

The first step was getting from neutral to first gear. It's embarrassing for me to admit how long it took me just to learn that part of the process. But even after I mastered this step, the car could not go more than 10 miles per hour in first gear. I eventually had to learn how to shift from first to second, and then from second to third.

It took a while, but shifting finally became a natural skill. Eventually Dad let me drive his car to my job, and I got to the point where I hardly had to think about what I was doing with the clutch, the brakes, and gearshift. Of course I was pretty busy honking at my friends or checking my hair in the mirror, but the driving part became fairly automatic.

Organizing the Past May Feel Like a New Skill to You

As we move through the buckets representing various aspects of your past, you too may feel as though you're learning how to drive a stick-shift vehicle. Constructing a biblical theology of the past may be new to you, but I hope by now you're feeling more comfortable with the process. You can organize the events from your past into biblical categories (or buckets, as we've called them). And you can apply Scripture to each category in a way that helps you empty the buckets in the sense that you have handled, or are handling, your part of the issue in a way that honors God.

In the last few chapters we have talked about times in your past when you were sinned against, and we learned there are two categories of responses: sometimes you responded well and other times you responded poorly. Thankfully, God's sufficient Word offers counsel for either response.

My prayer is that you can honestly say you are growing from your past; you have been organizing your past experiences into biblical categories and applying the appropriate principles from Scripture to each. I hope your testimony is that you are growing more in love with your Savior as you move through these steps. It's not simply a matter of *trying* to understand your past but of *using* your past to grow in your knowledge of Him (Philippians 3:8).

You May Be Halfway Done

When men and women consider their pasts through biblical categories such as these, they often discover a significant number of events or memories in each. If that's true in your case, and if you've been applying the principles and emptying buckets as you read along, you've made significant progress by now. Two of the four buckets are empty.

The basement's half clean. You've mastered second gear. You've lost half the weight you want to lose. This is not to suggest that the process won't continue in coming days as new events occur or new information becomes available. But to the best of your knowledge, you have dealt with these first two categories.

Now it's time to shift gears again. This next section of the book is about times in your past when you initiated the problem. Unlike your innocent past, now we're talking about times when you sinned first. There is no other way around it.

As was the case with the first two buckets, there is also the issue of your response. In some cases you sinned, but then you responded well. You quickly made things right with God and man, as Peter did after he denied Jesus. At other times you sinned, and then you sinned some more in your response, as David did in his relationship with Bathsheba. As we've seen all along, God's Word has powerful answers for each situation, but you have to organize each one first before you can apply the appropriate principles.

Why Does Bucket Three Even Exist?

You might wonder why we even need a Bucket Three. If you sinned, but then handled it properly by asking forgiveness of God and the people affected by your sin, why should this category of events and memories be an ongoing issue? That's a very good question. The truth is that many men and women feel stuck in their past even when they respond properly because they still struggle with these questions:

- What should I do if I don't feel forgiven?
- How should I respond when I keep remembering my failures?

I believe God's Word has compelling answers to these questions as well. Let's dig into the Scriptures and see how the Lord can help us empty Bucket Three. To do so, we'll have to learn the art of practicing *joyful remembrance.*

Understanding the Buckets

In what occurred, you were...

You responded...	INNOCENT	GUILTY
WELL	BUCKET 1 The innocent past when you responded well requires: **Authentic Suffering**	BUCKET 3 The guilty past when you responded well requires: **Joyful Remembrance**
POORLY	BUCKET 2 The innocent past when you responded poorly requires: **Humble Analysis**	

When You Do Not Feel Forgiven, Choose to Believe God's Promise

In several earlier chapters we discussed the important place emotions have in our Christian growth. God created us with the ability to feel deeply, and we should not ignore this aspect of what it means to be made in the image of God. However, our emotions are reliable only to the degree that they reflect biblical truth. That is why, for example, Jesus told the woman at the well, "God is spirit, and those who worship Him must worship in spirit and truth" (John 4:24). Our emotions must always be grounded in and directed by biblical truth.

After you have confessed your sin to God and to the appropriate people, the most important question to ask is not, "How do I feel?" Instead, you should focus on what God's Word has instructed you to believe about your status before Him, and what your Lord has done to make that status possible. Your eyes should not be on yourself and your sin but on the marvelous character of God.

God is a forgiving God

This is where our study becomes absolutely delicious: "O taste and see that the LORD is good; how blessed is the man who takes refuge in Him" (Psalm 34:8)! One of the emphases of Scripture is that God loves to forgive His children. God told the prophet Jeremiah that in spite of Israel's sin and rebellion and the just punishment they would experience as a result, a day was coming in which He would cleanse and forgive them:

> "I will cleanse them from all their iniquity by which they have sinned against Me, and I will pardon all their iniquities by which they have sinned against Me and by which they have transgressed against Me. It will be to Me a name of joy, praise and glory before all the nations of the earth which will hear of all the good that I do for them, and they will fear and tremble because of all the good and all the peace that I make for it" (Jeremiah 33:8-9).

Promises such as these are deeply imbedded in the Bible because they are a central aspect of the person of God. As we choose to believe God's promise to forgive us after we have sinned—regardless of how we feel—we are giving Him the honor due His name.

Jesus focused on forgiveness even while dying on the cross

Even while Jesus was dying for our sin to make forgiveness possible, He said of those who had mocked, ridiculed, tortured, and then crucified Him, "Father, forgive them; for they do not know what they are doing" (Luke 23:34). When we rejoice in the amazing cross-work of Christ after we have sinned, we are putting ourselves in a position to trust His unfailing character, not our unpredictable emotions.

God promises to forgive His children as soon as we come in repentance and faith

Earlier we studied one of the most blessed passages in Scripture, 1 John 1:9: "If we confess our sins, He is faithful and righteous to forgive us our sins and to cleanse us from all unrighteousness." Every second spent questioning this promise because of our unbelief is time that could have been devoted to marveling at our wonderful Lord. We should stand with people like the prophet Micah and ask,

> Who is a God like You, who pardons iniquity
> And passes over the rebellious act of the remnant
> of His possession?
> He does not retain His anger forever,
> Because He delights in unchanging love.
> (Micah 7:18)

This is why the Lord designed the table

Many changes have taken place through the centuries in how the followers of Christ have functioned in His church. But one constant among those who seek to use God's Word as their guide is to regularly observe the Lord's Supper (1 Corinthians 11:17-34).

This corporate observance of the people of God is the epitome of joyful remembrance. During this observance the focus is not on our sins alone, because we can look to something much greater than our failures—the sufficient blood of our Savior. Consider the following passages as representative of the beauty of His shed blood:

- "And when He had taken a cup and given thanks, He gave it to them, saying, 'Drink from it, all of you; for this is My blood of the covenant, which is poured out for many for forgiveness of sins'" (Matthew 26:27-28).
- "Much more then, having now been justified by His blood, we shall be saved from the wrath of God through Him" (Romans 5:9).
- "In Him we have redemption through His blood, the forgiveness of our trespasses, according to the riches of His grace" (Ephesians 1:7).
- "And through Him to reconcile all things to Himself, having made peace through the blood of His cross; through Him, I say, whether things on earth or things in heaven" (Colossians 1:20).

- "Therefore, brethren, since we have confidence to enter the holy place by the blood of Jesus" (Hebrews 10:19).
- "Knowing that you were not redeemed with perishable things like silver or gold from your futile way of life inherited from your forefathers, but with precious blood, as of a lamb unblemished and spotless, the blood of Christ" (1 Peter 1:18-19).
- "They sang a new song, saying, 'Worthy are You to take the book and to break its seals; for You were slain, and purchased for God with Your blood men from every tribe and tongue and people and nation'" (Revelation 5:9).

If you have struggled with feeling as though you have not been forgiven, why not jot down several of these verses on index cards? The next time this struggle arises, take out your cards and focus on what God has promised and what was necessary to secure your forgiveness. This will help you move from inadequate feelings to joyful remembrance.

When You Continually Rehearse Your Failures, Learn Not to Wallow in Sins of the Past

I pastor in the Midwest so I'm familiar with what it means to wallow. This is what pigs do in the mud, and they are incredibly adept at it. I realize this is not a pleasant metaphor, but people wallow too. You may know exactly what I'm talking about. We sin, then ask forgiveness of God and the appropriate people, but continue to relive our failure over and over. Our lack of spiritual progress makes a pig stuck in the mud look mobile in comparison. Something needs to be done.

What occurs in your mind is a choice of your will

You might be asking, "But how can I be held responsible for what I'm thinking? I cannot do anything to change my habit of reviewing my past failures." That is not true. God has created us with the ability to choose what we think about, and in Christ, we can train our minds to think thoughts that are pleasing to Him. Consider these verses:

- "Be renewed in the spirit of your mind" (Ephesians 4:23).
- "Whatever is true, whatever is honorable, whatever is right, whatever is pure, whatever is lovely, whatever is of good repute, if there is any excellence and if anything worthy of praise, dwell on these things" (Philippians 4:8).
- "Prepare your minds for action, keep sober in spirit, fix your hope completely on the grace to be brought to you at the revelation of Jesus Christ" (1 Peter 1:13).
- "Why are you in despair, O my soul? And why have you become disturbed within me? Hope in God, for I shall again praise Him for the help of His presence" (Psalm 42:5).

Why we become stuck in our past

You do not have to wallow around in the sins of your past; you do not have to review all the ways you failed. To get beyond this habit, you must discover what is occurring in your heart that makes it so easy for you to get caught up in this behavior. Here are four of the more prominent reasons men and women become stuck in their past by replaying their sin over and over in their minds:

1. a lack of genuine repentance
2. the fear of man
3. an unwillingness to forsake our sin
4. losing our awe of God's forgiving grace

These are serious issues in God's eyes not just because of the way they affect how we view our past sins, but because the presence of any of these habits can significantly hurt our walk with Christ. Let's take a closer look at each of these.

A lack of genuine repentance

In 2 Corinthians 7, the apostle Paul said there is a significant difference between worldly sorrow and godly sorrow:

> I now rejoice, not that you were made sorrowful, but that you were made sorrowful to the point of repentance; for you were made sorrowful according to the will of God, so that you might not suffer loss in anything through us. For the sorrow that is according to the will of God produces a repentance without regret, leading to salvation, but the sorrow of the world produces death (7:9-10).

The word *repent* means to turn around; to go the other way in your mind, in your heart, in your words, and in your actions. It means to turn yourself completely away from sin and go in the opposite direction toward righteousness.

The opposite of that is what Paul describes here as "worldly sorrow," which is a shallow substitute for the real thing. This is the person who is sorry because he got caught, not because he offended God. Or he's sorry he can't get away with his wrongdoing anymore, or sorry he's not going to be able to enjoy the pleasure of that sin any longer. People like that wallow in their sin; they replay the event over and over and wish they could find a way to do it again.

That is the crux of the issue: If you had the opportunity to sin in that way again, would you? If the answer is yes, then true repentance has not yet occurred. That was one of the problems with the people in the Corinthian church. They had a lot of teaching and many "showy gifts." But there was a shallowness to their faith that resulted in carnal living, broken relationships, and powerless ministry. Thankfully, because of Paul's letters, change was beginning to take place. There was sorrow to the point of repentance. If you don't sorrow in that way, you can't get out of Bucket Three because you'll continue to replay the sin over and over in your mind with the hope that you can somehow find a way to commit that sin again.

The fear of man

Earlier we saw that after we have asked for forgiveness, it's time to contemplate the magnificent character of our forgiving God. But some of God's people are transfixed on the possibility that people around them might know what they did. Proverbs 29:25 is very instructive on this point: "The fear of man brings a snare, but he who trusts in the LORD will be exalted."

A snare is used to trap or entangle wild animals. God uses that picture to describe human beings who are worried about gaining the approval of other people.

The bottom line is, after you have sinned and asked for forgiveness from God and the appropriate people, you should not continue to look around to find out who knows about what you did. You should instead look up to the God who has gloriously forgiven you because of His all-sufficient grace. "Where sin increased, grace abounded all the more" (Romans 5:20).

Some people have allowed the approval of others to become a powerful idol in their hearts. Their fear of other people finding out about the skeletons in their closets has caused them to jump from job to job, town to town, and church to church. What a terrible way for forgiven people to live!

If this describes you, I encourage you to pause and do business with the fear of man and the idol of craving the approval of others. "If God is for us, who is against us?" (Romans 8:31). Amen and amen. Paul concluded Romans 8 with these words:

> In all these things we overwhelmingly conquer through Him who loved us. For I am convinced that neither death, nor life, nor angels, nor principalities, nor things present, nor things to come, nor powers, nor height, nor depth, nor any other created thing, will be able to separate us from the love of God, which is in Christ Jesus our Lord (Romans 8:37-39).

Without a doubt one of the primary reasons some people are stuck in Bucket Three is that the fear of man motivates them to constantly rehearse past sins and worry about the approval of others. If that fear is in your heart, it's high time to put it out and replace it with joyful remembrance.

An unwillingness to forsake our sin

Within Proverbs 28:13 is a key phrase that helps us understand why we sometimes continue to relive our sins: "He who conceals his transgressions will not prosper, but he who confesses and forsakes them will find compassion." True confession and repentance have not occurred unless they are accompanied by steps to avoid that sin in the future. The phrase "and forsakes them" is one that's easily overlooked.

Jesus spoke about this in a startling way:

> "If your right eye makes you stumble, tear it out and throw it from you; for it is better for you to lose one of the parts of your body, than for your whole body to be thrown into hell. If your right hand makes you stumble, cut it off and throw it from you; for it is better for you to lose one of the parts of your body, than for your whole body to go into hell" (Matthew 5:29-30).

Jesus was speaking hyperbolically, but His point is clear: If you want to put past sins behind you, then you must take clear steps to avoid that sin in the future.

Losing our awe of God's forgiving grace

Some Christians seem to believe they need to repeatedly beat themselves up over past sins even after they have asked for God's forgiveness. It's almost as if they feel they must do some sort of penance to receive God's favor.

This approach to past failure is unbiblical. The apostle Paul himself had committed wicked atrocities before he became a Christian (Galatians 1:13-14; 1 Timothy 1:15-16), but he did not continue to wallow in them. Instead he rejoiced in God's grace (1 Timothy 1:12-17) and pressed forward to accomplish what God had planned for him today and in the future (Philippians 3:12-14).

Organizing the Past

In what occurred, you were…

	INNOCENT	GUILTY
You responded… WELL	BUCKET 1 The innocent past when you responded well requires: **Authentic Suffering** • ***Face it honestly.*** (Psalm 73:2—*But as for me, my feet came close to stumbling, my steps had almost slipped.)* • ***Face it biblically.*** (Psalm 73:17—*Until I came into the sanctuary of God)* • ***Face it hopefully.*** (2 Corinthians 1:3—*the Father of mercies and God of all comfort)* • ***Face it missionally.*** (2 Corinthians 1:4—*so that we will be able to comfort those who are in any affliction)*	BUCKET 3 The guilty past when you responded well requires: **Joyful Remembrance** • ***When you do not feel forgiven, choose to believe God's promise.*** (1 John 1:9) • ***When you continually rehearse your failures, learn not to wallow in sins of the past.*** – *Because of a lack of genuine repentance* (2 Corinthians 7:9-10) – *Because of the fear of man* (Proverbs 29:25) – *Because of an unwillingness to forsake the sin* (Proverbs 28:13) – *By losing our awe of God's forgiving grace* (Jeremiah 33:8-9)
You responded… POORLY	BUCKET 2 The innocent past when you responded poorly requires: **Humble Analysis** • ***Did you return evil for evil?*** (Romans 12:17-21) • ***Did you develop bitterness toward God?*** *(like Naomi in the book of Ruth)* • ***Did you develop an unbiblical view of people?*** (Matthew 22:37-40—*the second great command)* • ***Did you develop an unbiblical view of yourself?*** (Romans 12:3) • ***Should you have confronted the abuser and if so, have you?*** (Matthew 18:15-18) • ***If you confronted the abuser and he requested forgiveness, have you granted it?*** (Ephesians 4:32)	

For You

In this chapter, we have engaged the clutch and shifted into third gear. You may have unfinished business in Bucket Three, the guilty past where you responded well. If so, consider what is hindering you from resolving this. Perhaps you have allowed your feelings to control whether you believe God kept His promise to forgive you. Or maybe you've been mindful of your sin over and over even after you confessed it to God. Believe this—joyful remembrance is within your grasp. The beauty of getting there is worth the effort.

For Jill

Dealing with Bucket Three was a critical step toward overcoming Jill's depression. You may recall that before she came for counseling, she said, "I have acceptance issues." Jill would say today that this may have been the understatement of her life.

Where's my approval?

As we unpacked Jill's depression, she told us that her relationships with other people were strained. In the providence of God, Jill still had regular contact with her biological father. But she often gauged the success of those interactions on whether he gave her the approval she thought she deserved or needed.

If Jill walked into a room where her father was and he did not greet her affectionately, Jill took that as purposeful rejection. She would then brood for days and weeks about what she perceived to be ongoing slights. Is there any wonder she was depressed?

Some counselors might have scheduled a conversation with Jill's parents and encouraged them to be more complimentary to their daughter. I thought about doing that, but later realized that would be unwise in her case. Jill had made the approval of people a powerful idol. She derived her identity from the praise of others, and when they did not come through, she was devastated. Simply asking the people in Jill's life to treat her better would not transform the fundamental nature of her heart.

Jill's hunger for approval from people caused her relationship with the Lord to become distant. Her life was all about her performance. Because she believed she did not measure up in the eyes of others, she rehearsed her failures endlessly. This cycle of despair had a grip on her discouraged heart.

But God's Word is powerful, and Jill was truly ready to change. She came to see that she was living in the fear of others and allowing their approval of her to be a controlling idol. She needed instead to bask in God's forgiveness. As she came to understand and appreciate how her Savior's blood had cleansed her from her sin, she was able to rejoice in His unconditional love for her. Whenever she remembered past failures she had already confessed to God and others, she instead focused on the joy she received from remembering what Christ had done for her. She no longer purposely recalled her past sins, and when they came to mind, she didn't dwell on them. She learned to practice the skill of joyful forgiveness.

In the providence of God, at this point in the counseling process Jill's biological father asked her to accompany him to a family reunion. This would serve as a test of Jill's progress because she and her father would ride in the same car together for hours and because they were going to visit extended family members she barely knew.

Jill took the admonition of 1 Peter 1:13 to heart and began to "prepare [her] mind for action." Instead of worrying about all the ways she might be slighted by others, she planned how she would rejoice in Christ and then serve her father and other family members. We had several counseling sessions before the trip, and Jill was able to become excited over the opportunities God would give her to apply His Word and trust in Him. As a counselor, I sat back and marveled at the power of our God. He was transforming Jill from a woman who craved the approval of people to a woman who basked in the forgiveness and acceptance of her Savior.

Not surprisingly, there were a few rough spots during the trip. But Jill was quick to ask her father's forgiveness before anything got out of hand, and then she rejoiced in the knowledge that her Savior had forgiven her the moment she confessed her sin. Her father's approval was no longer her functional god.

I wish you could have seen Jill's face at the appointment after the trip. We had what amounted to a worship service as we marveled at God's power and willingness to transform idolatrous hearts.

Questions for Personal Reflection

1. Do you struggle with not feeling forgiven? What are some events from your past for which this is especially true?
2. Is the blood of Christ precious to you? When you happen to think about a past sin, what steps can you take to practice the art of *joyful remembrance?*
3. Do you ever wallow in your past sins? Can you relate to any of the reasons for this tendency that were mentioned in the chapter? What should you do now?

Questions for Group Discussion

1. Ask group members to describe an event that fits into Bucket Three. How does this event relate to the concept of being stuck in the past?
2. Discuss why *joyful remembrance* can sometimes be so elusive.
3. Brainstorm ways each member of the group can make the Lord's Supper a more meaningful and helpful experience. How can this contribute to the art of practicing joyful remembrance?

Case in Point Three

Learning to Embrace God's Forgiveness: A Picture of Joyful Remembrance

"You're under arrest." Those were the words Will heard when the door opened to the apartment he visited after arranging an immoral and illegal contact on the Internet. Like a car hitting a concrete wall at 80 miles per hour, Will's heart went from being consumed with lust to facing harsh reality in a millisecond. He had arrived with hopes of fulfilling his fantasies; instead, he was handcuffed by a police officer and taken to jail.

Will had planned and committed an act that would now become part of his guilty past. Although he was a follower of Christ and was married to a wonderful Christian woman, he had foolishly and willfully violated God's clear commands about marriage. There was no way to erase what he had done.

What would Will do next? He had to decide whether to respond like Peter, who after denying Christ, quickly and thoroughly repented of his wrong, or like David, who after committing adultery did further sins.

I met with Will and his wife, Lynn, within 24 hours of his arrest. His wife had bailed him out of jail, and they were sitting in my office wondering what they should do next. Eventually Will would spend seven months in prison for his crime, so there were several immediate legal issues we had to discuss. But the most pressing question was whether

Will would begin moving toward the Lord, his wife, and his church in repentance and faith, or run away in rebellion, shame, or pity.

We all have ways we have displeased God. But wise men and women choose to handle their sin as quickly and completely as possible. This is what differentiates Bucket Three from Bucket Four. And this is what Will chose to do.

The following is an interview with Will and Lynn. Rejoice with them in the glory of God's forgiveness and His incredible power to restore relationships that have been devastated by sin.

What was going through your mind during the first few minutes after your arrest? What emotions did you feel in those moments?

Will: My first thoughts were fear based. Will Lynn divorce me? Will the church remove me from membership and the ability to worship and fellowship there? Will I lose my job? What will my family think? Those sorts of thoughts were racing through my mind.

I was a wreck emotionally and felt completely alone. I couldn't stop shaking because I was so nervous and scared. The only thing I knew I could rest upon was that God is sovereign and in control. No matter what, I wasn't alone and I could talk to Him. There was no doubt in my mind He was there with me throughout the whole process. I was blessed with very kind and gentle officers and detectives who treated me respectfully.

You had to decide whether you were going to take responsibility for your actions or begin blaming them on others. Was that a challenge for you? Describe what occurred in your heart in the first few hours.

Will: Taking responsibility didn't come naturally or easy. I am ashamed to admit that my first reaction was to blame Lynn. But after talking with her and discussing my actions in the course of counseling, God showed me that I was fully responsible for my actions. Through those means, God revealed the areas where I had failed and needed to repent.

First, I asked for God's forgiveness for sinning against Him. I spent a lot of time reflecting on my actions—not only what occurred that day, but everything surrounding my habitual sin in the year and a half leading up to that moment. It was abundantly clear that my actions had created this mess. I had a lot of time to talk over my situation with

God and ask Him for strength to make it through this trial and ask for His abounding grace and mercy. I also recommitted my life to Him. I believed that was of utmost importance. It was the very least I could do to show my obedience to Him and reliance on Him.

Where were you when you received the call that Will had been arrested? What was that like for you? What were you thinking and feeling?

Lynn: I was at work, 15 minutes from the end of my day. I hadn't received a call from Will at lunch like I normally do, so when the phone rang I thought it was him calling me later than usual. Little did I know how much my life was about to dramatically change.

I thought it was a joke at first, but the officer put Will on speakerphone and confirmed that he had truly been arrested. I felt as if I'd been hit with a ton of bricks. I got off the phone and just started sobbing in my office. I didn't know what to do, and I knew I couldn't make it through this on my own. After I had somewhat pulled myself together, I called one of my most trusted friends from church, Stella. She said that she was coming to meet me so she could stay with me and help me make it through the evening. She also immediately started reminding me of biblical truth. That helped me begin to get a grip on what was occurring.

I kept telling myself that this wasn't possible, that there is no way Will would intentionally hurt me or ruin our lives. I needed some answers, and I knew I needed to talk to Will so I could make decisions about how I would respond. I was sad and frustrated and angry and hurt all at the same time.

When you and Will met with Steve for counseling, you were already beginning to ask for counsel about how God wanted you to respond. How did you get to the place where you were willing to think about this situation through the lens of forgiveness and restoration?

Lynn: I think what started me down the road to viewing this situation through the lens of forgiveness and restoration was the way Stella dropped everything to come help me the day Will was arrested. She continued to remind me of biblical truth all through the evening while we worked through the process of bailing Will out of jail. She just refused to allow me to go down the road of telling myself lies. I also think bailing Will out of jail and talking to him about the situation helped to answer my questions about whether he was who I thought he was or this crime actually represented who he was and he had been fooling me all those years. I was reminded of all the sins God has forgiven me of, and in light of that I couldn't do anything but forgive Will.

Describe what was occurring in your relationship with God during the first few days and weeks after your arrest. What verses and concepts from Scripture were especially helpful to you?

Will: For the first time in a long time, my relationship with God was deepening. I was in His Word daily and gleaning nuggets of truth that helped me deal with and prepare for the future trials. The day after I was arrested, one of the pastors from church called me and talked with and prayed for me. He also encouraged me to read and study Psalm 51, which was David's prayer after his affair with Bathsheba, and that helped me to understand God's mercy and grace. Other concepts that helped me were that I was a child of God and nothing could change that; sin is sin in God's eyes; and God has forgiven me even if no one else has.

Will, because this event was reported in the media, the church asked you to come before the church family and ask their forgiveness. Lynn, you stood by Will's side when he did that. Describe that event. Do you feel like your church family has modeled God's forgiveness in the way they have treated you? Have you remained in the same church family?

Lynn: We both were very nervous. But we had already spoken to several friends between Will's arrest and the time he publicly requested forgiveness from our church family. Some of our closer friends in the church had already forgiven Will and reminded us that we all sin and are in no place to judge one another.

It was a relief to publicly ask the church for forgiveness. The way our church does it, Will went up in front of the congregation during a Sunday evening service and asked for the church's forgiveness for not representing the church in a godly way before our community. Will wasn't asked to give additional details about his crime because that was no longer the focus. Then the church family was asked to stand if they were willing to forgive him—we don't think anyone remained seated! Talk about a tear-jerker evening!

Yes, our church family has modeled God's forgiveness! Will says that besides inside our home, it's the only other place where he knows he won't be judged for what he did. Yes, we have remained in the same church family.

You were eventually incarcerated for your crime. How did that period of time affect your relationship with God? How did it affect your relationship with your church family?

Will: It helped to strengthen my relationship with Him. He was the only one I could lean on, and I knew He would be there no matter what.

Also, I would say that in some areas my imprisonment had no effect on my relationship with the church family. In other ways, it strengthened my relationships. Many people from the church took time out of their busy workweeks to visit me and spend time encouraging me in my incarceration to continue to grow and witness to others. Many others wrote letters and cards encouraging me. And after I was released from prison, many people were excited to have me back in the body and made me feel at home again.

Lynn, what was it like for you while Will was incarcerated? How would you describe your interactions with the people in your church family? How did you avoid expressing self-righteousness in your dealings with Will when you visited him in jail/prison?

Lynn: It was kind of like when I was on co-op during college when I lived alone, but at the same time it was different because I had never lived in our house alone. We bought our house after we were married, so I didn't know it without him there. It was very strange to sleep in our bed alone. It was also overwhelming to bear responsibility for the duties of two people. I had to decide what obligations were the most important and let other things go until Will was released. I had the blessing of a couple of families allowing me to stay with them while

Will was incarcerated, which helped me not remain alone and helped me not to focus on myself or wallow in self-pity.

I had a lot of people ask me how I was doing when they saw me on Sundays or Wednesday evenings, and my response was usually, "Great, considering." I was determined not to let what was going on keep me from being joyful, reaching out to others, and serving my perfect and faithful God. I still had so much to be thankful for and praise God for even though this was a less-than-ideal situation. I had so many friends who were willing to help me and meet any needs I had. During this time I saw who my true friends were. Some friends stopped talking to us, but other people I didn't know all that well stepped up and are now good friends of ours.

Visiting Will while he was incarcerated was interesting. It was hard for me because I had no way to make sure Will was okay every day and that people were being nice to him, but God took care of that by giving Will a couple of brothers in Christ to watch out for him. God also gave Will favor in the eyes of a few of the corrections officers, and they treated him with dignity and respect, which is not a common thing. I was and still am amazed at God's awesome provision during that time.

I didn't have time to indulge in feelings of self-righteousness while Will was incarcerated because I was so busy keeping everything together (paying the bills, taking care of the house, working, serving at church). In fact, I'm not sure I struggled with self-righteousness. Rather, I struggled most with anger and resentment because Will had selfishly and foolishly thrown our life as we knew it down the drain so that he could momentarily pleasure himself. He had done that instead of thinking about others and how his actions would affect not only me but both our extended families.

Every time I start to think of all the sacrifices I've made and continue to make to keep our lives together, I'm reminded by Scripture that I can never do too much. My service to God and my sanctification will never be complete on this earth. I am commanded to continually die to myself, and stopping is not an option. So when I think

I've died to myself enough times, I'm reminded that there is no such thing as enough times. So I guess in that sense you could throw self-righteousness into the mix of sinful attitudes I've struggled with in relation to this situation.

You will never forget this event. But God has given you the strength to preserve your marriage and even grow in your relationship with Him and each other. Do you believe you've "grown from your past"? In what ways?

Lynn: I know that I have grown from my past. I don't treat sin as lightly as I used to, nor do I ignore the evidence of habitual sin. I also believe that God can use any circumstance for our good and His glory. It has been exciting to see how He's used this event already—one of Will's cell mates has accepted Christ as his Savior as a result of this, and we've given encouragement to another man Will met while in prison—and I look forward to witnessing the ways in which He will use it in the future. God continues to change me so that I'm not so judgmental. He is also making me into a more loving and compassionate person.

Will: I truly believe that I have grown from my past. I also don't treat sin as lightly as I once did. I'm more aware of the effects my thoughts have on my actions. I'm more aware of what my eyes see and how that affects the way I think. I spend more time taking my thoughts captive for Christ and lifting up my struggles to God.

I also desire to share more openly with Lynn when I'm struggling. This experience has also brought me to a place where I don't think I am better than other people. During my incarceration, I met a variety of people, and I no longer see them as "those guys in prison," but as people who need a Savior as much as I do. I by no means have it all figured out. I continue to seek God's guidance daily to help me grow and change to become more like Christ. That's a lifelong process that's challenging, yet it has many rewards.

Chapter Eleven

The Person of Our Joy

NOT LONG AGO I DROVE with my wife and children through the neighborhood where I grew up. It was yet another reminder of the power of the past. As soon as I turned the corner onto the street where my family lived when I was young, those 40-year-old memories came flooding back. Many of the thoughts were about great times I had with the other guys in the neighborhood.

At the end of the street was a three-way stop known as "the triangle," where we spent countless hours playing three-man baseball. My neighbor's front lawn was our football field. This was long before computers or video games. We went outside practically every day and played together until the sun went down. It was a blast. Many of my childhood recollections are filled with joy.

After You Clean Your Room

In regard to my playtime, my mom had one important rule—I could go out and play only *after* I had cleaned my room. I can't say that I found housework particularly attractive as a young boy, but I did it as quickly and thoroughly as I could because I wanted to get outside and enjoy the time with my friends.

In a sense we have followed a similar rule in this study. Working through the events represented by the first three buckets has not been easy. And what comes next in chapter 12 about Bucket Four will prove challenging as well. So let's pause at this point in our discussion and consider some key questions:

- What is the point of emptying the buckets anyway?
- What happens during the process of handling my past biblically?
- What should I expect after the buckets are empty?
- Why should I try to handle my past this way?
- What might I miss if I decide not to grow from my past?

Taking the time and energy to face formerly unaddressed issues in the past is like cleaning your room. The purpose of this chapter is to answer the question, What does "afterward you can go out and play" look like?

Empty Buckets Lead to a Fountain of Joy

This book is not primarily about a process; it's about a person—God Himself. My greatest concern is not that you learn a series of biblical principles or even take a few steps of behavioral obedience. Ultimately, God offers us the possibility of experiencing a vibrant, joyful relationship with Him. Unfinished business in the past will rob us of the delight we can find in Christ. To fully enjoy Him, we must clean our room.

In at least one way, my analogy about playing outside falls short. Cleaning my room and playing outside were sequential and mutually exclusive. I couldn't clean my room as I was playing outside—and the cleaning had to come first. However, God offers you the possibility of finding joy in Christ *as* you handle past events in a biblical fashion. In addition, the more you grow from your past, the greater your potential joy in Christ. Empty buckets lead to a fountain of joy.

A thirsty woman with a sordid past

Another Bible passage that demonstrates the power and centrality of a person's past is John 4, the story of the woman at the well. The text begins with the curious statement that Jesus "had to pass through Samaria" (John 4:4). Pastor and author John Piper explains the significance of Samaria:

> The Samaritans were leftovers from the northern Jewish kingdom who had intermarried with foreigners after the chiefs and nobles were taken into exile in 722 BC. They had once built a separate worship place on their own Mount Gerizim. They rejected all the Old Testament except their own version of the first five books of Moses. Their animosity toward Jews (such as Jesus) was centuries old.[1]

Jesus was tired from His journey, so He sat down by a well. And when a Samaritan woman came to draw water, Jesus asked her for a drink. The woman was stunned and said, "How is it that You, being a Jew, ask me for a drink since I am a Samaritan woman?" (John 4:9).

There is someone you do not yet know

The conversation becomes even more intriguing when the Lord responds, "If you knew the gift of God, and who it is who says to you, 'Give Me a drink,' you would have asked Him, and He would have given you living water" (v. 10).

The woman does not immediately get the point. So Jesus backs up and says it a different way: "Everyone who drinks of this water will thirst again; but whoever drinks of the water that I will give him shall never thirst; but the water that I will give him will become in him a well of water springing up to eternal life" (vv. 13-14).

Predictably, the woman responds, "Sir, give me this water, so I will not be thirsty nor come all the way here to draw" (v. 15). She saw Jesus' offer as an opportunity to save herself a lot of work.

There is something about your past you need to face

But then the conversation suddenly goes a new direction when our Lord says, "Go, call your husband and come here" (v. 16). Why did Jesus say that? Consider a point Christ made several verses earlier:

"Everyone who does evil hates the Light, and does not come to the Light for fear that his deeds will be exposed" (3:20). Jesus wanted the Samaritan woman to recognize the depth of her spiritual thirst, as indicated by her five marriages and the fact she was currently living with a man who was not her husband. Her emptiness needed to be exposed. She needed to clean her room.

That's what we've been doing in the previous chapters as we've considered a number of ways we can address events from our past. In many cases, that involved exposing sin. Having sin exposed is never a pleasant experience. It wasn't pleasant for the woman at the well, nor is it for you and me. But often that is the first step to growing from our past.

The price of misplaced worship

The woman then attempted to take the conversation in a different direction: "Sir, I perceive that You are a prophet. Our fathers worshiped in this mountain, and your people say that in Jerusalem is the place where men ought to worship" (4:19-20). In the providence of God, that is exactly where Jesus wanted the discussion to go. He wanted this woman to understand that her sinful life was the result of an idolatrous heart.

That pinpoints one of the hardest aspects of the bucket-emptying process. Idolatry of the heart is difficult to admit, but it is often at the core of our struggle. For example, a man who returns evil for evil may be worshipping the idol of revenge. He thinks about it, plans it, perhaps even dreams about it because revenge is his god. Or the woman who chooses the path of bitterness may be worshipping the idol of always being treated fairly. She believes that the secret to joy is finding ways to make people do what she wants at all times.

Yes, the woman at the well had a worship problem, and so do we. The number of idols available at Vanity Fair is a long and varied list.

As you have contemplated what growing from the past looks like in your life, you may have come face-to-face with desires and idols of the heart that you needed to confess to God and others. While taking that step is extremely difficult, it is also like placing a stick of dynamite at just the right place in a logjam. Confession at the deepest levels is necessary before we can begin to heal and grow.

You cannot enjoy the living water Jesus offers until you acknowledge the presence of broken cisterns. That was the terminology God used with His people in the Old Testament.

> "For My people have committed two evils:
> They have forsaken Me,
> The fountain of living waters,
> To hew for themselves cisterns,
> Broken cisterns
> That can hold no water."
>
> (Jeremiah 2:13)

Perhaps you can relate to those two evils as you have contemplated past actions that revealed a heart of misplaced worship.

The sufficiency of our Messiah

Jesus then explained to the Samaritan woman that God is Spirit, and people who wish to worship Him must do so in spirit and in truth. The woman said, "I know that Messiah is coming (He who is called Christ); when that One comes, He will declare all things to us" (4:25). The Lord's next words get at the very heart of the issue: "I who speak to you am He" (v. 26).

The fountain of life is not a religious system or a set of behavioral standards—it is a person, the Lord Jesus Christ. You want to keep your buckets empty so you can fill them to overflowing with a vibrant and joyful relationship with your God. John Piper explains:

> God is not unresponsive to the contrite longing of the soul. He comes and lifts the load of sin and fills our heart with gladness and gratitude. "You have turned for me my mourning into dancing; you have loosed my sackcloth and clothed me with gladness, that my glory may sing your praise and not be silent. O Lord, I will give thanks to you

> forever!" (Psalm 30:11-12)...In the end the heart longs not for any of God's good gifts, but for God Himself. To see Him and know Him and be in His presence is the soul's final feast. Beyond that there is no quest. Words fail. We call it pleasure, joy, delight. But these are weak pointers to the unspeakable experience..."In your presence there is fullness of joy; at your right hand are pleasures evermore" (Psalm 16:11).[2]

Believing that Christ is the Living Water and that you can find abundant joy in Him should serve as your primary motivation for handling your past biblically. We could discuss other motivations for sure, but this is the most important one. The process looks like this:

- You determine that unaddressed sin in the past has been a shallow substitute for the joy available in Christ. The broken cisterns of idolatry have failed you miserably.
- You also come to believe that Jesus will sustain you and give you joy as you deal with unresolved issues His way.
- Just as Jesus was willing to endure the cross "for the joy set before Him" (Hebrews 12:2), you take the challenge of emptying your buckets so you can develop a richer, fuller, more intimate relationship with your Savior.

Joy for Those Who Have Suffered

Let's test our theory on those who have struggled with suffering in the past. As we learned in previous chapters, some men and women feel too ashamed to ask legitimate questions about God during times of suffering. Others ignore their pain because they believe statements such as "Big boys don't cry," and "Time heals all wounds." Some respond to abusive treatment by sinning against the person who offended them. Is it truly possible to find joy by facing our suffering head-on as well as our response to it? The answer all through Scripture is a definite yes.

The joy of finding refuge in Him

Consider the following verses:

- "Let all who take refuge in You be glad, let them ever sing for joy; and may You shelter them, that those who love Your name may exult in You" (Psalm 5:11).
- "You will make known to me the path of life; in Your presence is fullness of joy; in Your right hand there are pleasures forever" (Psalm 16:11).
- "You have been my help, and in the shadow of Your wings I sing for joy" (Psalm 63:7).
- "'Come to Me, all who are weary and heavy-laden, and I will give you rest. Take My yoke upon you and learn from Me, for I am gentle and humble in heart, and you will find rest for your souls. For My yoke is easy and My burden is light'" (Matthew 11:28-30).

Have you noticed we are often most motivated to take refuge in God when we are suffering? When we move toward Him instead of away from Him in times of hurt, we find joy and intimacy that is available only to those who have suffered well. Cleaning our room of wrong responses to past hurts paves the way for us to experience a richer walk with Christ. We find His yoke easy and His burden light because we are moving forward together with Him. In His presence is the fullness of joy.

The joy of seeing Jesus answer your prayers

Immediately prior to His death, Jesus told His disciples, "Until now you have asked for nothing in My name; ask and you will receive, so that your joy may be made full" (John 16:24). What an incredible promise! Because of our trust in the finished work of Christ, we have assurance that we will receive abundant answers to our prayers. As we walk through our suffering hand in hand with our Savior, we will experience fullness of joy as we watch Him answer our prayers.

This is one of the reasons cleaning the room of your past makes so much sense. All your former idolatry could never provide this joyful intimacy with the very Son of God. Have you ever felt truly joyful after you blew up at a person who treated you in an abusive way? Did you say a few days later, "I'm so glad I cursed like that—I wish I had used fouler language"? I doubt it. But when you choose to use your lips to cry out to God as you suffer, you experience a kind of joy that is available only in Him.

The joy of watching the Holy Spirit develop His fruit in you

The past is so troubling to many men and women because it is filled with what Scripture refers to as "deeds of the flesh." One classic passage on this topic is Galatians 5:19-21, where Paul said, "Now the deeds of the flesh are evident, which are: immorality, impurity, sensuality, idolatry, sorcery, enmities, strife, jealousy, outbursts of anger, disputes, dissensions, factions, envying, drunkenness, carousing, and things like these."

You might look at that list and think, *Paul has been reading my mail!* Perhaps God has been reading your heart. But the good news is you don't have to struggle over your past deeds of the flesh. You truly can clean your room. The even better news is you don't have to clean it alone. Paul went on to say, "But the fruit of the Spirit is love, joy, peace, patience, kindness, goodness, faithfulness, gentleness, self-control; against such things there is no law. Now those who belong to Christ Jesus have crucified the flesh with its passions and desires. If we live by the Spirit, let us also walk by the Spirit" (Galatians 5:22-25).

This is the fruit *of the Spirit.* You don't have to manufacture it on your own or conjure it up by human effort and wisdom. Notice that part of the Spirit's fruit is joy. As you develop love, peace, patience, and so on, you will also experience joy. Your heart will fill with joy as you witness the changes God makes in you.

A careful reader might ask, "Well then, am I cleaning my room or is God doing it?" The answer is both. You have to fulfill your responsibility, and God will certainly fulfill His. "Work out your salvation with fear and trembling; for it is God who is at work in you, both to will and to work for His good pleasure" (Philippians 2:12-13). But the Holy

Spirit stands ready to give you a kind of joy that is found only in tapping into the resources of heaven.

Is cleaning our room hard? You bet it is. But the result is true and lasting joy as the Holy Spirit blesses our efforts to obey God.

The joy of experiencing spiritual victory

Some people don't want to deal with their past because it is filled with failure. They believe any attempts to untangle the mess will just result in more misery and heartache. As a result, they never experience the joy that comes from allowing God to give them spiritual victory.

- "We will sing for joy over your victory, and in the name of our God we will set up our banners. May the Lord fulfill all your petitions" (Psalm 20:5).
- "Be glad in the Lord and rejoice, you righteous ones; and shout for joy, all you who are upright in heart" (Psalm 32:11).
- "Sing for joy in the Lord, O you righteous ones; praise is becoming to the upright" (Psalm 33:1).

One of my earliest counseling cases involved a husband and wife who often resorted to fistfights to solve their problems. They had recently come to Christ, but no one had taught them how to solve their differences in a Christ-honoring way. The primary reason they came to see me was that the level of violence in their home was continuing to escalate. A recent fight had resulted in significant physical injuries to both of them.

When they came in for their first session, they were physically trembling. When I asked what was going on emotionally, they explained that they were afraid they were going to seriously hurt each other. Theirs was a complicated case for sure, but it was exciting to see God bring change to their lives.

I distinctly remember the day they came in and told about how he had bought a car without asking for her input. Within days the car broke down, and he found himself in the street in front of their house trying to fix the problem. This happened in the middle of the winter.

He told me, "I looked out from under the car and saw her feet." Normally that would have begun the fight as she ridiculed him for the foolish decision he had made.

He balled his fists and slowly pushed his way out from under the car, ready to do battle yet again. But instead of a brawling wife, he found a loving spouse standing there with a hot cup of coffee and a plate of warm cinnamon rolls. She said; "Honey, I know it's cold out here, and I just wanted to make something to warm you up. Is there anything I can do to help?"

I wish I had a video of their faces in that session. They had finally experienced victory because they had handled the situation God's way. That simple act of putting on the Spirit's fruit of love gave them more joy than all their previous sinful responses combined. They did not know Psalm 20:5 at that point in their journey, but their expressions said it all: "We will sing for joy over your victory, and in the name of our God we will set up our banners." Jesus Christ had given them a win.

Suffering is never easy—that's a given. But if we have unfinished business in this area of our life, we need to look out the window and see the triangle where I played baseball or the neighbor's football field. The joy that is available afterward makes cleaning our room worth the effort, especially because our joy is not in a game but in a person.

Joy for Those Who Have Sinned

Let's switch gears and go to the other side of the equation. What about those whose sin initiated the problem? Much of what we have already studied could apply here as well, but certain aspects of spiritual joy are especially sweet to those who have blown it in the past.

The joy of learning God's Word

Thinking about how to address and overcome failure in the past should drive us to the Scriptures. And what do we find as we embark on this process? Drudgery? Lifeless principles? Moralism? Not at all. God's people find joy in learning His truth.

- "I have inherited Your testimonies forever, for they are the joy of my heart" (Psalm 119:111).
- "Your words were found and I ate them, and Your words became for me a joy and the delight of my heart; for I have been called by Your name, O LORD God of hosts" (Jeremiah 15:16).

I love it when counselees tell me that their knowledge of and love for God's Word has increased dramatically.

"Now we understand God and His will for us so much better."

"Now we have a much more vibrant walk with Christ."

"Now we know what steps to take when problems arise."

Getting to that place is never easy because it involves work, effort, and diligent study (2 Timothy 2:15). The desire to know freedom from our past troubles can motivate us to take those difficult steps. The result of replacing a bucket of past troubles with a bucket of biblical truth is genuine joy.

The joy of solving problems

Are you the kind of person who hates confrontation? I have learned over the years that many people will go to great lengths to avoid sitting down with another person and discussing a problem with the goal of finding a biblical solution. They live by one of the following mantras:

- Joy comes from ignoring problems.
- Joy comes from gossiping behind the other person's back.
- Joy comes from cutting this person off and finding a new friend.
- Joy comes from buying something I don't need instead of facing this problem.
- Joy comes from eating more than I should instead of facing this problem.
- Joy comes from boozing it up instead of facing this problem.

You get the picture. However, God's Word tells a different story. There is only one source of joy and freedom from our past problems, and that is the truth of God's Word. Any solution that contradicts Scripture leads to sure defeat.

Consider the case of Euodia and Syntyche, two women in the church at Philippi who were at odds with each other. Paul wrote a letter to their church from prison, a letter that emphasized the possibility of finding joy regardless of one's circumstances. Apparently the problems between these two women were publicly known because Paul chose to directly call them out in this letter. Please keep in mind that these epistles were typically read out loud to the whole congregation. Here's what Paul said:

> My beloved brethren whom I long to see, my joy and crown, in this way stand firm in the Lord, my beloved. I urge Euodia and I urge Syntyche to live in harmony in the Lord. Indeed, true companion, I ask you also to help these women who have shared my struggle in the cause of the gospel, together with Clement also and the rest of my fellow workers, whose names are in the book of life (Philippians 4:1-3).

Paul went on to give a strong exhortation to live in a joyful manner. However, in Euodia and Syntyche's case, that joy would come only *after* they had worked out their problems with each other.

Earlier in his letter Paul had hinted at this problem when he said, "Make my joy complete by being of the same mind, maintaining the same love, united in spirit, intent on one purpose" (2:2). Paul had such a strong relationship with this church that his joy was not complete until they did everything they could to develop Christian unity. That is why he reminded them, before bringing up the problem with these two ladies, that he considered them to be his "joy and crown." But that joy was diminished for him, for these two women, and for the entire church family until they settled their differences.

As you studied the earlier chapters in this book, you may have determined that part of the unfinished business in your past included an unsolved problem with another person. If that is the case, I hope you took the time to contact the person—provided it was appropriate to do so—and tried to make things right. I imagine that if you did, you would say it was one of the hardest steps you have ever taken. But I also believe that regardless of the way the other person responded, if you made the effort to obey God in this matter, He undoubtedly rewarded you with joy.

The joy of practicing genuine worship

Allowing idolatry to go unchecked is an exhausting and depressing way to live. The idols of our hearts demand much and provide little.

Recently I worked with a man who loved booze. His alcohol was destroying his marriage and everything else in his life. He was miserable, and so was everyone else. But he tenaciously held on to his idol.

At a pivotal point in our conversation, with his wife present, I asked him point blank: "Who do you love more, your booze or your wife?" His silence revealed the answer we all suspected and feared. Then I asked, "Who do you love more, your booze or your God?" The silence was deafening.

Compare that to the words of the psalmist: "I will go to the altar of God, to God my exceeding joy; and upon the lyre I shall praise You, O God, my God" (Psalm 43:4). Empty buckets lead to the possibility of true, joyful worship. You can become like the woman at the well, who found Jesus to be a "well of water springing up to eternal life" (John 4:14). He and He alone is worthy of our joyful worship.

When this counselee affirmed the idolatrous nature of his heart, I was reminded of the words of C.S. Lewis:

> If we consider the unblushing promise of reward and the staggering nature of the rewards promised in the Gospels, it would seem that our Lord finds our desires not too strong, but too weak. We are half-hearted creatures, fooling about with drink and sex and ambition when infinite joy is offered us, like an ignorant child who wants to go

> on making mud pies in a slum because he cannot imagine what is meant by the offer of a holiday by the sea. We are far too easily pleased.[3]

That is the point of this chapter. The great joy that is available in Christ should motivate us to handle whatever unfinished business in the past is hindering the full development of our relationship with Him. Let's work hard to empty our buckets so that we can fill them at the fountain of joy.

You can go out and play...*after* you clean your room!

Questions for Personal Reflection

1. List some ways that handling the past poorly resulted in the absence of joy for you.
2. How would you rate yourself on finding your joy in Christ? Is this a reality in your life? Explain your answer.
3. Do you agree that spiritual victory results in joy? What are some of the times you have found this to be true in your life?

Questions for Group Discussion

1. Brainstorm various ways our unwillingness to handle issues of the past robs us of the joy available in Christ.
2. What prevents us from "cleaning our rooms" more quickly and completely?
3. Reread C.S. Lewis's quote at the end of the chapter. Ask various members of the group to describe how and why it is so easy to be satisfied making mud pies in a slum.

Chapter Twelve

Honest Self-Confrontation: Reaching into Bucket Four

Practically every boy who grew up in our neighborhood played baseball at Longfellow Little League. It was a big deal. They had uniforms, an opening-day parade, high-quality fields, and a skill-graded system of denim, minor, and major leagues. Did I mention that they had uniforms? I didn't think about it much at the time, but looking back, I now realize that a large group of adult men and women must have worked behind the scenes to organize such a great program.

One spring I was at a transition point between leagues. Guys my age who were fairly good ballplayers would be chosen by Longfellow major league coaches to play on their teams. They had the best athletes, the better attended games, and of course the nicer uniforms. In my neighborhood, being chosen for a major league team was a significant event. The players who were not as good were doomed to another year in the minors. I don't want to overstate the case, but my entire life and future were on the line.

The coaches determined who would play on major league teams after a Saturday morning tryout. The problem was, I was never a very good athlete. I guess I could have blamed the problem on my genes (none of my ancestors played baseball) or my environment (my dad disliked sports). But the truth was, I was petrified of failure in general and of being hit by the ball in particular. Yet I was also competitive, and I really wanted to wear one of those nicer uniforms, so I asked my dad to take me to the tryout.

It was a beautiful spring day. The sky was blue, the air was crisp, and I was scared out of my mind. The first stage of the tryout determined which boys might have pitching skills. I knew I wasn't a good pitcher and I quickly proved it after throwing several wild pitches way over the coach who had squatted down behind home plate. At one point my dad asked me, "Son, are you *trying* to hit the catcher's mitt?" That was okay though—I knew I would fail that part of the tryout, and I did.

Next came batting. That wasn't exactly a strong suit of mine either. I tried to overcome my fear of the ball, but I wasn't doing very well. It's hard to hit the ball when your eyes are closed. Sure enough, I let three perfect pitches go by without even swinging. Strike one—strike two—strike three—I was out! But that was still somewhat okay—I had known I probably wouldn't do very well at batting.

What I was relying on most was my skill in the outfield. I could catch fly balls, and I fully intended to prove that to the onlooking coaches and players. When my name was called, I confidently trotted to the outfield and scraped my new cleats on the turf. The coach hit a fly ball high in the air. I ran under it and positioned myself just right. Then at the last moment I lost the ball in the bright sun. I started to duck my head, but it was too late. The ball hit me on top of my head and bounced away. I was completely humiliated. Not only had I failed at pitching and batting—I had even failed at fielding!

I was the Charlie Brown of Longfellow Little League.

Does That Sound Familiar?

Most of us recognize ourselves in that story because we've all had experiences where we failed multiple times. And such failure affects us not only in the physical realm, but the spiritual realm as well. That is the essence of Bucket Four. We sinned, and then to top it off, we sinned again.

- Like the husband who reacted in sinful anger, and then later blamed his anger on his wife's supposed failures.
- Like the person who spoke sinfully to her friend, and then cut off the relationship instead of asking forgiveness.
- Like the wife who overspent the budget, and then pouted when confronted about the problems that her choices created for the family.
- Like the man who looked at Internet porn at the office, and later blamed it on a coworker who shares his computer.
- Like the employee who was fired for subpar performance, and subsequently gossiped about his boss.

This brings us to Bucket Four—sinful behavior that was followed by a poor response. Failure followed by a failure. It's important for us to deal with this category of behavior and response; otherwise, we'll find ourselves perpetually stuck in the past. "He who conceals his transgressions will not prosper" (Proverbs 28:13). That is a promise of Scripture. The great news for those who handle multiple failures God's way is there is the potential of better days ahead.

Because sometimes you need to finish your stories right away

Are you wondering what happened after my failed Little League tryout? Amazingly, the next week the phone rang at our house, and it was the coach of Tip-Top, the local grocery store that sponsored the major league team with the best uniforms in the entire program. The coach informed my dad that he had chosen me for his team. I could not believe it. I was on Tip-Top! I was in the majors! I got to wear their orange and white uniform. In one phone call, I went from being Charlie Brown to Hank Aaron…for reasons I'll never be able to explain in this life.

Now let's turn to matters much more serious. What about the times in your past when you failed, and then you responded with additional sin? Perhaps you've tried to blame such failures on others. Or maybe you've gone to great lengths to hide what you have done. Perhaps you're avoiding the other person or trying to ignore what occurred. But deep inside, it's eating you alive. Past failures that are left unaddressed are like a slow-growing cancer of the soul.

Let's get this straight: The Coach knows. The Coach—He saw you miss the mitt. He saw you strike out. And then He saw the ball hit you on top of your head. Nothing escapes His gaze. He knows all the ways you have failed in the past.

But if you know Jesus Christ as Savior and Lord, at some point in your life your phone rang. The Coach wanted you on His team. "You did not choose Me but I chose you, and appointed you that you would go and bear fruit" (John 15:16). Don't try to make sense of it—His ways don't always make sense (Isaiah 55:8-9). But now it is time to act on the implications of the call. It is time to look at the uniform. It is time to honestly face any events still in Bucket Four and put them to rest. Let's let Scripture help us do that.

One of the best yet saddest examples of Bucket Four failure is the story of David and Bathsheba. We considered this event briefly back in chapter 4. If you haven't read this account recently, I encourage you to take out your Bible and carefully read 2 Samuel 11:1–12:25. In this passage we find four principles that can help us deal with sin quickly and completely. Otherwise, we will only complicate matters by making further wrong choices. Doing this requires practicing *Honest Self-Confrontation.*

Understanding the Buckets

In what occurred, you were…

You responded…	INNOCENT	GUILTY
WELL	BUCKET 1 The innocent past when you responded well requires: **Authentic Suffering**	BUCKET 3 The guilty past when you responded well requires: **Joyful Remembrance**
POORLY	BUCKET 2 The innocent past when you responded poorly requires: **Humble Analysis**	BUCKET 4 The guilty past when you responded poorly requires: **Honest Self-Confrontation**

Realize That Everyone Has Sin in Their Past

I am not suggesting that every person has sinned as wickedly as David did. But Scripture clearly states that "if we say that we have no sin, we are deceiving ourselves and the truth is not in us" (1 John 1:8). Keep in mind that David is mentioned in the New Testament as a "man after God's own heart" (Acts 13:22). If David, a man after God's own heart, was capable of significant sin in the past, so are we.

Sin begins by not controlling your desires

David's encounter with Bathsheba occurred in the spring of the year, "at the time when kings go out to battle" (2 Samuel 11:1). Scripture does not explain why David did not accompany his troops. But the fact he stayed behind is what led to trouble. While walking on his rooftop, he looked out over the housetops around him. There he saw Bathsheba, the wife of Uriah, bathing. Uriah was one of David's military captains. The text does not give us any indication that David or Bathsheba had done anything wrong at this point in the story—it very well may have been an innocent action on her part and an unplanned glance by him.

Everything now hinged on what "desire of the heart" David would choose next. One of the most helpful passages in the Bible when seeking to understand human motivation is James 1:13-15:

> Let no one say when he is tempted, "I am being tempted by God"; for God cannot be tempted by evil, and He Himself does not tempt anyone. But each one is tempted when he is carried away and enticed by his own lust. Then when lust has conceived, it gives birth to sin; and when sin is accomplished, it brings forth death.

David could have chosen any number of proper desires the moment he saw Bathsheba bathing:

- I *want* to be loyal to my friend Uriah, who is currently serving me on the field of battle.

- I *want* to do everything I can to promote the health and vitality of Uriah and Bathsheba's marriage union.
- I *want* to follow the example of Job, who made a covenant with his eyes and refused to look at a maid in a lustful manner (Job 31:1).
- I *want* to show how much I love God by delighting in Him (Psalm 37:4) rather than the sinful lusts of my heart.
- I *want* to cry out to God for help in overcoming this temptation so I can find strength and endurance at His throne (Psalm 61:1-2).

This is why it's so important for us to "discipline [our] mind for action" and "take every thought captive to the obedience of Christ." That terminology comes from two precious passages in God's Word:

> Therefore, prepare your minds for action, keep sober in spirit, fix your hope completely on the grace to be brought to you at the revelation of Jesus Christ. As obedient children, do not be conformed to the former lusts which were yours in your ignorance, but like the Holy One who called you, be holy yourselves also in all your behavior; because it is written, "YOU SHALL BE HOLY, FOR I AM HOLY" (1 Peter 1:13-16).

> We are destroying speculations and every lofty thing raised up against the knowledge of God, and we are taking every thought captive to the obedience of Christ (2 Corinthians 10:5).

Practicing honest self-confrontation requires a more comprehensive analysis than simply acknowledging our wrong behavioral choices. This entire sordid event in David's life could have ended in one verse had he simply chosen to think something like, *I just saw something I should not have seen, and I sensed a desire that did not honor God. But now I am going to crucify that lust and replace it with a godly desire before this goes any further.*

If you and I are ever going to truly empty Bucket Four, we will have to become skilled at honestly confronting our tendency to follow the lusts of our hearts.

Do not complicate matters by acting on the wrong thoughts and desires of your heart

Your mind is a buffer between you and the other parts of your body and between you and the other people in your life. That's important to remember because if you do battle there, you can shut down the process of sin before it progresses to outward actions that can harm you and others.

Regrettably, David chose to act on his lusts:

- "So David *sent* and *inquired* about the woman" (2 Samuel 11:3, emphasis added).
- "David *sent* messengers and *took* her" (2 Samuel 11:4, emphasis added).

As you witness David's actions, you might find yourself wanting to scream, "David, what were you thinking?" The truth is, at this point he wasn't thinking—at least not in a godly fashion. He was acting on the lusts of his heart in a way that was practically animalistic.

Though we may find David's actions disappointing, we can also identify with him. We too have experienced times in the past when we chose to move forward with desires, thoughts, and actions that dishonored our God. Some of those failures make being hit on top of the head with a baseball seem mild in comparison.

The pleasure of sin is brief compared to its effects

The Bible is no cheap romance novel. The only description of David's actual act with Bathsheba is summarized in four words: "he lay with her" (2 Samuel 11:4). That is not because God is a prude—in other places where marital love is celebrated, such as the Song of Solomon, the descriptions are extended and beautiful. But not here, because lust always produces death (James 1:15). Whatever pleasure David received from this atrocity is quickly diminished by the result: "The woman conceived; and she sent and told David, and said, 'I am pregnant'" (2 Samuel 11:5).

The Key Question Is—How Did You Respond After You Sinned?

This is where the story becomes especially sinister. Instead of facing his sin and accepting the consequences, David chose to add more sin to the heap. He sent a message to the front lines and asked that Bathsheba's husband, Uriah, return to give David a report of the battle. David assumed that Uriah would also go home and enjoy the beauty of appropriate sexual love with his wife. However, Uriah showed himself to be a far more honorable man than David when he said,

> "The ark and Israel and Judah are staying in temporary shelters, and my lord Joab and the servants of my lord are camping in the open field. Shall I then go to my house to eat and to drink and to lie with my wife? By your life and the life of your soul, I will not do this thing" (2 Samuel 11:11).

This brings us to a series of questions we need to ask about our response to sin in the past. Think of these questions not only as they relate to David's subsequent steps after his sin with Bathsheba, but also in the way you tend to respond when you have failed.

Did you try to cover it up?

The only way a situation can make it to Bucket Four is when we sin and fail to handle it properly right away. One reason we might give for letting the problem get out of hand is that it is hard to ask forgiveness and make restitution. We avoid doing what's right because it's so difficult. But consider all the effort we often put into covering up our sins. In David's case, it would have been far easier for him had he responded to his sin quickly instead of trying to cover it up. That is true for you and me as well.

Did you plan steps you never would have considered before?

David attempted to cover his sin of adultery by committing the sin of murder. When Uriah did not have sexual relations with Bathsheba, David orchestrated a surefire way for Uriah to get killed in battle.

This part of the story demonstrates the sheer insanity of sin. Solomon, a child of David and Bathsheba, would eventually write, "The hearts of the sons of men are full of evil and insanity is in their hearts throughout their lives. Afterwards they go to the dead" (Ecclesiastes 9:3). The longer you leave an event in Bucket Four, the more likely you are to consider actions you never would have contemplated when your heart was closer to the Lord.

Have you let your sin make you callous to its effects on others?

"When the wife of Uriah heard that Uriah her husband was dead, she mourned for her husband" (2 Samuel 11:26). Imagine the grief Bathsheba must have experienced. Remember, she was also expecting a child at the time.

The passage is silent about whether David expressed any remorse for how his actions affected Bathsheba. Instead we read, "When the time of mourning was over, David sent and brought her to his house and she became his wife" (2 Samuel 11:27). How exactly did that work? He sent and asked? He sent and demanded? Did Bathsheba have a say in the matter? Did David care?

This is another consequence of allowing events to stay in Bucket Four. A person can be so consumed with covering his tracks that he is completely oblivious to how his actions damage the lives of others.

Beware of Significant Consequences for Not Dealing with Sin Quickly

One of the primary reasons men and women leave past sins unaddressed is that they believe they can get away with it. At some point, David believed his plan had worked.

However, the God of heaven always has the last say. "The thing that

David had done was evil in the sight of the Lord" (2 Samuel 11:27b). David should have heeded his own counsel:

> O Lord, You have searched me and known me.
> You know when I sit down and when I rise up;
> You understand my thought from afar.
> You scrutinize my path and my lying down,
> And are intimately acquainted with all my ways.
> (Psalm 139:1-3)

The Bible has many admonitions about the importance of addressing sin right away:

- "Be sure your sin will find you out" (Numbers 32:23).
- "The way of transgressors is hard" (Proverbs 13:15 KJV).
- "Do not be deceived, God is not mocked; for whatever a man sows, this he will also reap" (Galatians 6:7).

Months elapsed before the consequences began to unfold. God sent the prophet Nathan to tell David about a rich man with many lambs who took a poor man's only lamb by force. David was outraged and declared that the rich man should be put to death, or at least should have to restore the lamb fourfold. Then Nathan looked right into David's eyes and said,

> "You are the man! Thus says the Lord God of Israel, 'It is I who anointed you king over Israel and it is I who delivered you from the hand of Saul. I also gave you your master's house and your master's wives into your care, and I gave you the house of Israel and Judah; and if that had been too little, I would have added to you many more things like these! Why have you despised the word of the Lord by doing evil in His sight? You have struck down Uriah the Hittite with the sword, have taken his wife to be your wife, and have killed him with the sword of the sons of Ammon'" (2 Samuel 12:7-9).

How do you think the "joy" David received from his sin compared to the consequences he and others eventually experienced?

Unaddressed guilt

Many students of Scripture believe that Psalm 38 and 51 were written between the time David sinned and the time Nathan confronted him. These passages help us understand what it feels like when we leave events in Bucket Four:

> Your arrows have sunk deep into me,
> And Your hand has pressed down on me.
> There is no soundness in my flesh because of
> Your indignation;
> There is no health in my bones because of my sin.
> For my iniquities are gone over my head;
> As a heavy burden they weigh too much for me.
> My wounds grow foul and fester
> Because of my folly.
> I am bent over and greatly bowed down;
> I go mourning all day long.
> For my loins are filled with burning,
> And there is no soundness in my flesh.
> I am benumbed and badly crushed;
> I groan because of the agitation of my heart.
> (Psalm 38:2-8)

> I know my transgressions,
> And my sin is ever before me.
> Against You, You only, I have sinned
> And done what is evil in Your sight,
> So that You are justified when You speak
> And blameless when You judge.
> (Psalm 51:3-4)

Destruction to your family

Through the prophet Nathan, God explained to David that "the sword shall never depart from your house, because you have despised Me and have taken the wife of Uriah the Hittite to be your wife" (2 Samuel 12:10). The Bible goes on in detail about the deaths of four of David's sons, three of whom were killed in battle.

The Lord then said, "I will raise up evil against you from your own household; I will even take your wives before your eyes and give them to your companion, and he will lie with your wives in broad daylight. Indeed you did it secretly, but I will do this thing before all Israel, and under the sun" (12:11-12). These words were tragically fulfilled by the debased actions of David's son Absalom (16:1-2).

The passage ends with the heartbreaking story of the death of David and Bathsheba's little baby. While David expressed a long-range hope that he would see his baby again (12:23), the immediate devastation must have been overwhelming.

Do you have outstanding events in Bucket Four that you need to take care of? What are some of the possible consequences to you and others if you allow these actions to go unaddressed?

Rejoice Because There Is Hope for Getting Out of Bucket Four

David finally came to his senses. At least he did not make the mistake of ignoring Nathan's confrontation. He said, "I have sinned against the Lord" (12:13). Those simple but profound words began the process of emptying Bucket Four. David later wrote about the joy of forgiveness:

> How blessed is he whose transgression is forgiven,
> Whose sin is covered!
> How blessed is the man to whom the Lord does
>   not impute iniquity,
> And in whose spirit there is no deceit!
> When I kept silent about my sin, my body
>   wasted away

Through my groaning all day long.
For day and night Your hand was heavy upon me;
My vitality was drained away as with the fever heat
  of summer.
I acknowledged my sin to You,
And my iniquity I did not hide;
I said, "I will confess my transgressions to the LORD";
And You forgave the guilt of my sin.
Therefore, let everyone who is godly pray to You in
  a time when You may be found;
Surely in a flood of great waters they will not reach
  him.
You are my hiding place; You preserve me from
  trouble;
You surround me with songs of deliverance.
(Psalm 32:1-7)

Organizing the Past

In what occurred, you were…

You responded…	INNOCENT	GUILTY
WELL	BUCKET 1 The innocent past when you responded well requires: **Authentic Suffering** • ***Face it honestly.*** (Psalm 73:2—*But as for me, my feet came close to stumbling, my steps had almost slipped.*) • ***Face it biblically.*** (Psalm 73:17—*Until I came into the sanctuary of God*) • ***Face it hopefully.*** (2 Corinthians 1:3—*the Father of mercies and God of all comfort*) • ***Face it missionally.*** (2 Corinthians 1:4—*so that we will be able to comfort those who are in any affliction*)	BUCKET 3 The guilty past when you responded well requires: **Joyful Remembrance** • ***When you do not feel forgiven, choose to believe God's promise.*** (1 John 1:9) • ***When you continually rehearse your failures, learn not to wallow in sins of the past.*** – *Because of a lack of genuine repentance* (2 Corinthians 7:9-10) – *Because of the fear of man* (Proverbs 29:25) – *Because of an unwillingness to forsake the sin* (Proverbs 28:13) – *By losing our awe of God's forgiving grace* (Jeremiah 33:8-9)
POORLY	BUCKET 2 The innocent past when you responded poorly requires: **Humble Analysis** • ***Did you return evil for evil?*** (Romans 12:17-21) • ***Did you develop bitterness toward God?*** *(like Naomi in the book of Ruth)* • ***Did you develop an unbiblical view of people?*** (Matthew 22:37-40—*the second great command*) • ***Did you develop an unbiblical view of yourself?*** (Romans 12:3) • ***Should you have confronted the abuser and if so, have you?*** (Matthew 18:15-18) • ***If you confronted the abuser and he requested forgiveness, have you granted it?*** (Ephesians 4:32)	BUCKET 4 The guilty past when you responded poorly requires: **Honest Self-Confrontation** • ***Realize that everyone has sin in their past.*** (1 John 1:8, 10—*If we say that we have no sin, we are deceiving ourselves*) • ***Understand that the key question is—How did you respond after the event?*** (2 Samuel 11:3-4) • ***Beware of significant consequences for not dealing with sin quickly.*** (Numbers 32:23, Proverbs 13:15) • ***Rejoice because there is hope for getting out of bucket 4.*** (Psalms 32:1-7)

For You

We have all missed the mitt, struck out, and dropped the ball. David's story is our story in that we don't always handle our sins properly and quickly. This is one of the primary reasons we get stuck in the past.

If that is true of you in any way, why not begin the steps of honest confrontation? If you need to ask God's forgiveness, there's no better time than now to get on your knees and talk to Him. If you need to ask forgiveness from others, then pick up the phone or schedule a time to meet and make things right. You may even have to make restitution or face significant consequences. But David is right: "How blessed is he whose transgression is forgiven, whose sin is covered."

For Jill

Early in the counseling process, Jill reported that her mother had signed Jill over as a ward of the state because she believed Jill was incorrigible. As our counseling progressed, Jill concluded on her own that in many ways her mother had been correct. There were numerous examples of how she had been displeasing to God as a daughter, especially in her teenage years. This did not excuse the sin of her mother or other family members. But it did mean that Jill had things in Bucket Four that needed addressing.

By this time Jill was secure enough in her relationship with Christ to practice honest self-confrontation. She listed the ways she had sinned against her parents and eventually asked God and her parents for forgiveness.

The impact this had on Jill's emotional state was dramatic. She was thinking and speaking the truth about her past. Because she knew her sufficient Savior would forgive and cleanse her, she courageously acknowledged ways she had sinned (1 John 1:9). She no longer needed to run, hide, or blame her sin on others. This did not mean she took more responsibility for past problems than truly belonged to her—but she was no longer willing to take any less. Jill's experience mirrored

David's: "How blessed is the man to whom the Lord does not impute iniquity" (Psalm 32:2).

Emptying Bucket Four also paved the way for a new approach to relating to others, even those who had failed Jill in the past. The restoration could now begin in earnest because she had confronted those who had sinned against her and asked forgiveness for the ways she had sinned against them.

In the sovereign plan of God, Jill's mother was having trouble paying her bills. I remember the day Jill came in and reported that she and her husband had discussed and prayed about whether this might prove a good opportunity for them to show love to her mom by allowing her to move into their basement apartment.

I asked Jill whether she would be able to relate to her mother in a consistently loving way in light of all that had occurred. But Jill and her husband believed that because she had dealt with the unfinished business from her past and grown significantly in her relationship with Christ, it was time to joyfully accept this challenge. So they worked together to prepare the apartment and helped her mother move in.

Jill's change was so dramatic that her mother eventually sought biblical counseling to work on some of the ways she needed to grow. Jill had gone from being incorrigible as a teenager to being encouraging as an adult. By God's grace, she had genuinely grown from her past.

Questions for Personal Reflection

1. What are some situations when you've sinned and then responded poorly?
2. Do you have anything that still remains in Bucket Four? What do you think you should do now?
3. What event from your past have you addressed recently? Was it hard to do so? Are you glad you did?

Questions for Group Discussion

1. Discuss as a group which was worse: David's adultery with Bathsheba or the way he chose to respond to this sin. What lessons can we learn from this observation?
2. Brainstorm the ways that we as Christians can do a better job of giving careful attention to the desires of our hearts.
3. Share prayer requests about specific ways each group member hopes to grow from his or her past.

Case in Point Four

Facing a Calloused Heart: A Picture of Honest Self-Confrontation

John grew up in a wonderful Christian home and married his college sweetheart. On the outside his life looked as if it were heading the right direction, but on the inside John's heart had grown cold to the things of God. This bled over into his relationship with his wife, and John eventually sought to fulfill his sexual desires outside his marriage.

When John's infidelity came to light, he had a choice to make. Unfortunately, he chose to face the disobedience in his past by attempting to run away from God. Eventually John was disciplined by his church and lost his wife.

But thanks be to God, "where sin increased, grace abounded all the more" (Romans 5:20). John spent several years living in Bucket Four. He pursued the pleasures of sin for a time, but ultimately found God's Word to be true. "Be sure your sin will find you out" (Numbers 32:23).

John was eventually reconciled to God. He then came before his church family and was restored to them as well. His story proves that while living in Bucket Four is a terrible existence, it does not have to remain permanent. He came to the place where he could say with the psalmist, "Great are Your mercies, O Lord; revive me according to Your ordinances" (Psalm 119:156). Here's John's story in his own words.

After your infidelity came to light, you had the choice of either moving toward the Lord or away from Him. You chose the latter. Why? What was going through your mind and heart in those days?

It seemed easier to quit than to work through the problems and start over again. I knew people could work through things like that and go on to become better, but it didn't seem worth the work. I knew I was wrong, but I was convinced it would be better for all involved.

Did you have contact with Christians during the time you were living in rebellion? What were those exchanges like?

I had contact with a couple of Christian friends, and my family kept in contact with me too. The general feel I got from these conversations was that these people loved me and wanted me to come back to Christ. Most conversations included at least one urging to return to church and repent.

When did you begin to change your mind about the direction you were heading? Were there any events, conversations, or concepts from Scripture that were especially helpful?

A friend of mine was diagnosed with a rare and particularly powerful form of cancer. From diagnosis to his death was about eight months. He was a godly man, husband, and father of two, active in his church and a picture of Christ to all who knew him. His wife blogged their experiences, and I saw how they handled difficulty by turning to Christ. I vividly remember wondering why God would let me live but take this man who was doing so much for Him. Shortly after his death, another friend emailed me about it, and that led to conversation about what I'd been doing over the past three years. That led to another encouragement to seek forgiveness while I still had opportunity.

I had known all along what the right course was, but I was embarrassed and full of pride. The events of that summer, combined with the weariness of trying to go my own way, led me to realize I needed to get things right.

What was the experience of restoration to God and forgiveness like for you?

Once I came to understand what actual forgiveness meant—both from God and from those I had hurt—I was dumbfounded. The pastor I was counseling with was very clear that my sin didn't make me a second-class spiritual citizen and that I was expected to grow and change and serve from that point on—just like anyone else in the church. It was unbelievable that after so gross a sin, they were willing to forgive and put me in a place of fellowship and service.

Part of your repentance involved going back to people you had sinned against and requesting forgiveness. Describe some of those interchanges. Are you glad now about what you did?

It was very difficult, but those I approached made it much easier by showing grace. I sat in the pastor's office across from my ex-wife and her new husband and very specifically asked her forgiveness for the many wrongs I had committed against her. She quickly and ecstatically forgave me, and it was evident that she had been burdened more for me than she was concerned about her own feelings of hurt and pain. I am certainly glad I asked for forgiveness. It's impossible for me to imagine where I'd be if I hadn't.

You also went before your church family and requested their forgiveness. Were they willing to forgive you? Have they been receptive to your involvement and participation since then?

After I read my statement in front of the church body and asked for forgiveness, the pastor asked all who were willing to forgive me to stand. He had me look out and see that everyone in the auditorium was standing. After the service, many, many people came up to me to hug me and welcome me back and praise God that I had been restored.

To say the church family has been "receptive" to my participation and involvement is an understatement, really. It is more accurate to say that my participation and involvement were expected. "Being restored," the pastor told me, "means working with the church family, getting back in the game."

What advice would you have for a person who is running from God today?

Turn around! If you haven't realized already that you've come to the end of yourself, you soon will. There is no hope in self; there is hope only in God. And while God is patient, you have no guarantee that His patience will continue. Turn around before it's too late!

Do you believe you have grown from your past? Is there any real hope for a person who messed up and then responded by messing up even more?

In many ways, I believe I've grown more from my mistakes than I have from any other circumstances. I'm much more aware of God's grace now, and I have learned the lesson that the ungrateful servant in Matthew 18 did not: I have been forgiven much, so I must be willing to forgive much. I understand more about how a person can fail by not paying attention to *every* step he takes. I hope these lessons stay with me for the rest of my life.

There's all kinds of hope for someone who has compounded his problems by making bad choices after bad choices. God is faithful to forgive! I have become fond of telling people that as long as we are alive, we still have the opportunity to seek forgiveness.

Epilogue

A Front-Row Seat in Theology Class

DURING MY SENIOR YEAR of Bible college, I took on far more responsibilities than my body would tolerate. I was working one part-time job to pay the remainder of my tuition bill. I had a second job because Kris and I were engaged, and I wanted to take her on a nice honeymoon after our wedding. I was carrying a full class load and was also serving as a part-time youth pastor on the weekends at a church in a neighboring state. Let's just say I was busy and there wasn't a whole lot of time for things like sleep.

That schedule eventually began to take its toll. I was not doing a good job at anything, including my course work. I tried hard to concentrate but found myself falling asleep in class all too frequently.

Sleeping in Theology Class

One day I was in the back row of theology class, a room that had cabinets and a countertop right behind the last row of chairs. Apparently I was resting my head on the countertop behind me and had fallen asleep.

By my friends' telling, the president of the college walked by our classroom, saw my posture, and stopped to watch for a while. Eventually he walked into our room, interrupted the professor, and asked if he knew there was a student sound asleep in the back. Because our college president had such a booming voice, I woke up just in time to hear the theology professor respond, "Yes, please let him sleep; he's better behaved that way." Over the years my friends have often reminded me of my stellar performance in that class.

An Invitation to Attend Theology Class Yourself

In a sense this book has been an invitation to theology class. Upon reading the word *theology,* please do not think of it as some stuffy academic knowledge that has no relevance to your life today. R.C. Sproul was right when he said,

> No Christian can avoid theology. Every Christian is a theologian. Perhaps not a theologian in the technical or professional sense, but a theologian nonetheless. The issue for Christians is not whether we are going to be theologians but whether we are going to be good theologians or bad ones.[1]

Handling your past properly provides many opportunities to learn exciting truths about God as you develop a more intimate relationship with Him. Failing to handle unaddressed issues in your past is like sleeping in theology class because you are missing many opportunities to learn more about God, His Word, and yourself. Having the courage to empty your buckets can bring you face-to-face with life-changing truths from Scripture.

As we conclude this study, consider what Jill learned because she was willing to do the hard work of facing and dealing with her past.

What Jill learned about God

We never used the phrase *theology proper* (doctrine of God) in our times together, but there was a direct relationship between the improvements in Jill's depression and her growing love for and knowledge of God. Jill had previously responded to her past in ways that distanced her from the Lord. Like many abuse victims, she frequently viewed her heavenly Father through the lens of what she had experienced with her earthly one.

Jill was similar to Naomi in the Old Testament book of Ruth. Both women had adopted the working theology that says, "The Almighty has dealt bitterly with me. I went out full, but the LORD has brought me back empty" (Ruth 1:20-21). But just like Naomi, God brought Jill to a place where her view of Him dramatically changed. She found Him to be a loving Father who stood ready to sustain, guide, heal, and forgive. Her testimony became that of the psalmist: "O taste and see that the LORD is good; how blessed is the man who takes refuge in Him" (Psalm 34:8).

Jill also saw her prayer life improve. She was learning, in the tradition of the apostle Peter, to cast all her care upon God, because she was becoming increasingly convinced that He cares for her (1 Peter 5:7). Jill would be the first to say this process needs to continue lifelong. And she is significantly encouraged that she is finally on the right road.

Have you allowed past challenges to teach you important lessons about the person and work of your God? Do you know Him and love Him more because you've been a good steward of your past? Are you committed to facing future challenges in a way that helps you continue to grow in your knowledge of God?

What Jill learned about herself

We also never used the word *anthropology* (doctrine of man) in our sessions, but Jill came to see that an underlying reason for her depression was her faulty view of what it meant to be human. It was a tremendous help to Jill to reflect on how she had been made in the image of God. She was not simply a passive victim who was being ruthlessly driven in directions beyond her control.

God made Jill for the powerful purpose of glorifying Him. She came to understand that she was a *worshipping being* capable of learning to love the Lord with all her heart, soul, mind, and strength.

Jill began to start her days with praising the Lord for all the blessings in her life. Her depression had blinded her to the many ways God had been good to her, including giving her a loving husband and wonderful children. Jill began trying to live each day with the goal of pleasing God (2 Corinthians 5:9) and becoming more conformed to the image of Christ (Romans 8:28-29).

The opportunity the Lord gave Jill to extend special grace to her biological mother became a profound test of Jill's new view of herself. She could have chosen to view herself through the eyes of her depression, disappointment, and hurts from the past. Instead she focused on the fact that, as a new person in Christ, she could demonstrate her love for her God by showing compassion to her mother who had sometimes failed her.

Has your view of yourself changed as you've read this book? Have you ever fallen into the trap of viewing yourself as a helpless victim? How do you intend to view yourself differently in the days ahead?

What Jill learned about sin

We did not use the word *hamartiology* (doctrine of sin), but we frequently discussed the power and presence of sin in the world we live in. Authentic sufferers acknowledge that this side of heaven, we must expect to face disappointment, abuse, and hateful treatment from others. Developing spiritual candor is an important skill because we will sometimes be called upon to say with the psalmist, "I am weary with my sighing; every night I make my bed swim, I dissolve my couch with my tears" (Psalm 6:6).

Jill was also willing to admit her past sins. At first this was new territory for her. But soon she began to experience the joy of repentance and confession. Her sin was as ugly as the rest of ours, but the fact she could cast it as far as the east is from the west (Psalm 103:12) became a powerful motivation for her.

This was especially true of the sins of Jill's heart. She had never contemplated the possibility that her wrong desires may have contributed to her negative emotional state. When she confessed she had allowed the approval of others to become a powerful idol, she uncovered an important explanation of what had occurred in her past.

Jill received great hope as she watched God help her replace the sinful desires of her heart with ones that honored Him. Jill learned to rejoice in her security in Christ and was freed up to serve others whether she received their approval or not.

This is where the biblical ideas behind the use of the four buckets we have been studying in this book became so helpful. Jill's past had been a confused jumble of events, hurts, decisions, memories, abuses, words, and actions. Some people in her life said everything in her past was her fault, while others believed none of it was. The truth was somewhere in between. The buckets allowed her to organize the events in her past into biblical categories, and then deal with any sin that she had committed.

Has this study encouraged you to acknowledge sin in the past? If so, I hope you have also taken the proper steps of repentance and confession to God and the appropriate people. God wants to help you deal with any past guilt so you can move forward with a clear conscience before Him.

What Jill learned about Christ

I did not say the word *Christology* (doctrine of Christ), but our discussions were decidedly Christ-centered. Jill was able to face both the suffering and sin of her past because she was developing a robust relationship with her crucified and risen Savior.

Jill's depression began to lift as she learned what it meant to live "in Christ." Ideas such as the sustaining gospel, our union with Christ, and the goal of greater Christlikeness stretched her theological understanding. Learning to apply these ideas to everyday life became a source of challenge and strength.

Jill's testimony began to mirror that of the apostle Paul, who expressed the desire to "know Him and the power of His resurrection and the fellowship of His sufferings, being conformed to His death" (Philippians 3:10). Jill's identity was no longer focused on her depression and abuse, but instead on the person and work of her Savior.

My prayer is that you too have been drawn closer to Christ as you've considered your past in light of God's Word. Why not join Jill and the apostle Paul in praying that you will continue to grow in your knowledge of Him?

What Jill learned about the Spirit

We didn't use the term *pneumatology* (doctrine of the Holy Spirit), but Jill learned the power of the Holy Spirit in the process of change. One of her biggest challenges was that she had felt all alone in her struggles. Imagine her joy when she reflected on verses such as Romans 8:11: "But if the Spirit of Him who raised Jesus from the dead dwells in you, He who raised Christ Jesus from the dead will also give life to your mortal bodies through His Spirit who dwells in you." Growing from her past was a big job—but now she was learning to draw on the power of the same Spirit who raised Jesus from the dead.

If you know Christ as Savior and Lord, the Holy Spirit lives inside you (1 Corinthians 6:19-20). He is your Helper, and according to the promise of Jesus Himself, will be with you forever (John 14:16). Be encouraged that you never have to face a difficulty in the past, present, or future alone.

What Jill learned about salvation and growth

I am certain we did not use the words *soteriology* (doctrine of salvation) or *progressive sanctification* (doctrine of Christian growth), but we often spoke about how the Redeemer could use Jill's past for her spiritual development. This gave Jill great hope for her struggle. As she focused on growing in Christ, she began to "consider it all joy...when you encounter various trials, knowing that the testing of your faith produces endurance. And let endurance have its perfect result" (James 1:2-4).

Each step of growth gave Jill additional hope and confidence. She was working out her own salvation, knowing that it was God who was at work in her, "both to will and to work for His good pleasure" (Philippians 2:12-13).

The Redeemer is also working out His plan in you. He wants to use trials from your past to help you develop endurance and spiritual maturity.

What Jill learned about eternity

No, we didn't use the word *eschatology* (doctrine of the end times) either, but Jill was also helped by viewing her circumstances in light of eternity. Verses such as these became a more prominent focus in her life:

- "I consider that the sufferings of this present time are not worthy to be compared with the glory that is to be revealed to us" (Romans 8:18).
- "Yet in a very little while, He who is coming will come, and will not delay" (Hebrews 10:37).
- "After you have suffered for a little while, the God of all grace, who called you to His eternal glory in Christ, will Himself perfect, confirm, strengthen and establish you" (1 Peter 5:10).

Depression narrows your focus. Jill learned to view her struggles as "a little while" compared to the glories of eternity.

You too can begin to view the difficulties from your past through the lens of eternity. You cannot erase your past suffering, but you can put it in its proper perspective.

Have You Been Asleep in Theology Class?

Perhaps you shook your head when you read about me falling asleep in theology class. It would seem that a person studying for the ministry should show greater diligence at every opportunity to learn truth about God and His Word.

The following summer Kris and I were married, and we were able to go on a great honeymoon to Bermuda, one of our favorite spots on earth. That fall, Kris took on a job so she could help put me through seminary. My attitude toward classes changed dramatically. I decided that if my wife was going to work to put me through school, I was going to get everything I possibly could out of my classes.

By God's grace, those theology classes became a great source of blessing to me. I had some tremendous professors, and often the classes were transformed into worship services as we considered God and His ways. I regret that it took me so long to appreciate the learning opportunities I had and to pay closer attention.

My prayer is that you will use what you've learned in this book to address any unresolved issues from your past. I hope you've discovered that you can sort out your past and take care of specific aspects of it with the help of truths from Scripture. Along the way, make sure you focus not simply on the principles of the Bible, but also on the person of our God.

As you do, you will truly grow as you put your past in its place.

Notes

Chapter 1

1. D. Martyn Lloyd-Jones, *Spiritual Depression: Its Causes and Its Cure* (Grand Rapids, MI: Wm. B. Eerdmans Publishing Co., 1965), 61.
2. John MacArthur, *Our Sufficiency in Christ* (Dallas, TX: Word Publishing, 1991), 223.
3. Albert Barnes, *Notes on the Old Testament: Psalms,* vol. 1 (Grand Rapids, MI: Baker, 1974), 171.

Chapter 2

1. Kenneth L. Barker and Waylon Bailey, *The New American Commentary,* vol. 20 (Nashville, TN: Broadman & Holman, 1998), 277-78.
2. Robert W. Kellemen, *Soul Physicians* (Winona Lake, IN: BMH Books, 2007), 300.
3. Wayne A. Mack and David Swavely, *Life in the Father's House* (Phillipsburg, NJ: P&R Publishing, 1996), 133.
4. S. Augustine, Bishop of Hippo, and E. B. Pusey, *The Confessions of St. Augustine* (Oak Harbor, WA: Logos Research Systems, Inc., 1996), Conf, book 8, chapter 5.
5. Ed Welch, *Addictions—A Banquet in the Grave* (Phillipsburg, NJ: P&R Publishing, 2001), 11-12.
6. Cornelius Plantinga Jr., *Not the Way It's Supposed to Be: A Breviary of Sin* (Grand Rapids, MI: Wm. B. Eerdmans Publishing Co., 1995).
7. C.H. Spurgeon, *New Park Street Pulpit,* vol. 1 (Grand Rapids, MI: Baker, 1990), 1.

Chapter 3

1. Elyse Fitzpatrick and Dennis Johnson, *Counsel from the Cross* (Wheaton, IL: Crossway Books, 2009), 30.

Chapter 5

1. Harold S. Kushner, *When Bad Things Happen to Good People* (New York: Anchor Books, 2004), 4.
2. Ibid., 4-5.
3. Ibid., 17-18.
4. Ibid., 37.
5. Ibid., 42-43.
6. Ibid., 48-49.
7. Ibid., 49.
8. Ibid., 147.

Chapter 6

1. Dustin Shramek, "Waiting for the Morning during the Long Night of Weeping" in *Suffering and the Sovereignty of God,* ed. John Piper and Justin Taylor (Wheaton, IL: Crossway Books, 2006), 175.
2. D.A. Carson, *How Long O Lord?* (Grand Rapids, MI: Baker Academic, 2006), 63.
3. Paul Tripp, *Suffering: Eternity Makes a Difference* (Phillipsburg, NJ: P & R Publishing, 2001), 6.
4. Richard Baxter, *The Saints' Everlasting Rest* (Grand Rapids, MI: Baker, 1978), 246.
5. Philip Edgcumbe Hughes, *Paul's Second Epistle to the Corinthians,* New International Commentary on the New Testament (Grand Rapids, MI: Wm. B. Eerdmans Publishing Co., 1962), 11.
6. Piper, *Suffering and the Sovereignty of God,* 82.
7. Tripp, *Suffering,* 24.

Chapter 7

1. Ed Welch, *Motives: Why Do I Do the Things I Do?* (Phillipsburg, NJ: P & R Publishing, 2003), 23.
2. C.J. Mahaney, *Living the Cross-Centered Life* (Colorado Springs, CO: Multnomah Books, 2002), 25.

3. Milton Vincent, *The Gospel Primer for Christians* (Bemidji, MN: Focus Publishing, 2008), 5.
4. C.H. Spurgeon, *Morning and Evening* (Peabody, MA: Hendrickson Publishing, 1991), January 4 evening meditation.
5. Vincent, *Gospel Primer,* 39-40.
6. D.A. Carson quoted in Mahaney, *Living the Cross-Centered Life,* 98.
7. Spurgeon, *Morning and Evening,* January 11 evening meditation.

Chapter 8

1. C.S. Lewis, *The Abolition of Man* (New York: HarperCollins, 1974), 1, 11.
2. A.W. Tozer, *The Knowledge of the Holy* (New York: HarperCollins, 1961), 1.

Chapter 11

1. John Piper, *Desiring God* (Colorado Springs, CO: Multnomah Books, 1986), 78.
2. Ibid., 87.
3. C.S. Lewis, *The Weight of Glory and Other Addresses* (Grand Rapids, MI: Wm. B. Eerdmans Publishing Co, 1965), 1-2.

Epilogue

1. R.C. Sproul, *Knowing Scripture* (Downers Grove, IL: InterVarsity Press, 1977), 22.

Overcoming Fear, Worry, and Anxiety: Becoming a Woman of Faith and Confidence

Elyse Fitzpatrick

Elyse Fitzpatrick, coauthor of *Women Helping Women,* offers practical advice for conquering the paralyzing emotions many women encounter as they battle difficult, often overwhelming concerns about rebellious children, problems in the workplace or home, health issues, financial difficulties, and more.

In the Bible, God gives guidance and offers the true solution to our anxieties and fears. *Overcoming Fear, Worry, and Anxiety* accesses this information to help women—

- identify the source of fear, worry, and anxiety
- transform fearful thoughts into peaceful confidence
- discover specific strategies for overcoming anxiety

Women will find comfort and encouragement through real-life examples of how others, including Elyse, cast their cares upon God and experience His strength and love.

Elyse Fitzpatrick is the head of Women Helping Women Ministries and holds an MA in biblical counseling from Trinity Theological Seminary. She has authored more than a dozen books, including *Love to Eat, Hate to Eat.* She and her husband, Phil, have three grown children as well as grandchildren.

Women Counseling Women: Biblical Answers to Life's Difficult Problems

Elyse Fitzpatrick

Multitudes of women struggle daily with negative habits and addictions, emotions such as anger and depression, various kinds of loneliness, and other difficulties experienced by mothers, wives, or singles.

Here is a rich counseling resource that looks to the Bible alone as being sufficient to address our every need. Author Elyse Fitzpatrick and several contributors are all qualified biblical counselors skilled at interweaving the perfect wisdom of God's Word with heartfelt compassion and concern for those who need help. Among the topics are…

- emotions, worry, and depression
- eating disorders and habitual struggles and sins
- grief and caregiving

Designed for both self-use and as a guide for counseling others, *Women Counseling Women* offers answers that will encourage and endure because God's Word is timeless and full of wisdom for the problems women face.

Women Helping Women: A Biblical Guide to Major Issues Women Face

Elyse Fitzpatrick and Carol Cornish

A resource for women who desire to help other women. For each major life issue covered there's a concise overview, a clear biblical perspective, and practical guidelines from experts. Women will be encouraged as they discover how God's Word changes hearts.